The Climate Action Monitor 2024

OECD
BETTER POLICIES FOR BETTER LIVES

Please cite this publication as:
OECD (2024), *The Climate Action Monitor 2024*, OECD Publishing, Paris, https://doi.org/10.1787/787786f6-en.

ISBN 978-92-64-71031-3 (print)
ISBN 978-92-64-48920-2 (PDF)
ISBN 978-92-64-84839-9 (HTML)
ISBN 978-92-64-44042-5 (epub)

The Climate Action Monitor
ISSN 2958-1591 (online)

Photo credits: Cover © M. Federico/Shutterstock.com; © Bilanol/Shutterstock.com; © Scott Book/Shutterstock.com; © Jan Tolar/Shutterstock.com.

Corrigenda to OECD publications may be found at: https://www.oecd.org/en/publications/support/corrigenda.html.

Preface

The impacts of climate change continued to be felt this year. Increasing global average temperatures are intensifying climate-related hazards and risks, resulting in significant and unpredictable outcomes, moving us closer to potentially crossing irreversible climate tipping points. Countries have an opportunity to address this challenge, by implementing comprehensive and ambitious commitments in the next round of Nationally Determined Contributions in February 2025.

The findings in this edition of the International Programme for Action on Climate (IPAC) Climate Action Monitor show that current commitments have not been matched with effective action. The OECD's Climate Action Policy Measurement Framework (CAPMF) shows that climate policy action, measured as a combination of policy adoption and stringency, expanded by 10% on average each year over the 2010-2021 period. In 2022 and 2023, this expansion slowed to 1% and 2% respectively. More effective, robust climate policies are needed.

Current greenhouse gas (GHG) emission targets, even if fully implemented, are not ambitious enough to achieve the reductions necessary to achieve the Paris Agreement's temperature goals. To limit the rise in average global temperature to 1.5 degree Celsius above pre-industrial levels, the International Panel on Climate Change (IPCC) estimates that a 43% reduction in global emissions is needed by 2030. Greater ambition must also be matched with a better coordinated approach to ensure the sustainable transition is both globally effective and fair.

This year's United Nations Framework Convention on Climate Change (UNFCCC) Conference of Parties (COP29) is an opportunity to enhance ambition and enable climate action. Building on the OECD's multidisciplinary expertise, IPAC contributes to global climate action by providing comparable and harmonised information to monitor national and global climate action. Towards this, the Climate Action Monitor provides key indicators related to GHG emissions trajectories and targets, trends in climate-related hazards, and progress on global climate action.

Enhanced climate ambition and action, underpinned by sound tracking of commitments and progress, will be essential to achieving our climate goals, and ultimately enabling a more sustainable and inclusive future for all. The OECD will continue to actively support this effort through our data and analysis.

Mathias Cormann,

OECD Secretary-General

Foreword

The Climate Action Monitor summarises climate policy action centred on 50 countries and the EU covered under the International Programme for Action on Climate (IPAC), offering policy makers and practitioners a comprehensive overview of trends.

Established in 2021 by the OECD Ministerial Council Meeting, IPAC seeks to facilitate progress towards achieving net-zero greenhouse gas emissions and establish a more resilient economy by mid-century. Overseen by the OECD Environment Policy Committee, IPAC forms an integral part of the OECD's strategy to incorporate climate action across all its work, harnessing a multidisciplinary and whole-of-economy approach.

To support global objectives, IPAC equips governments with an indicator dashboard and analytical reports. This enables the monitoring, evaluation and assessment of climate action using data sourced from official channels or validated by countries. Nonetheless, complete information on all countries and policies is not yet available. The challenge in the coming years is to develop a coherent, consistent and comprehensive set of indicators to help countries accelerate their transitions towards net zero.

Drawing on a vast array of international climate-related data, indicators and studies devised collaboratively with the International Energy Agency, the International Transport Forum, the Nuclear Energy Agency and the United Nations Framework Convention on Climate Change, IPAC encompasses the environmental, economic and social dimensions of climate change. The data presented are based primarily on indicators developed by IPAC and on analytical research by the OECD and sister organisations.

This report, authored by Rodrigo Pizarro, Mikaël J.A. Maes, Daniel Nachtigall, Edoardo Falchi and Pinhas Zamorano, builds on data collected by Carla Bertuzzi, Max Böhringer, Salvatore Finizio, Mauro Migotto, Santaro Sakata, Andrzej Suchodolski, Jiwon Choi, Bopha Chun and Laura Elizabeth Smith. The work was conducted under the supervision of Nathalie Girouard, Head of the Environmental Performance and Information Division in the OECD Environment Directorate. Natasha Cline-Thomas, Fiorella Cianchi, Beth Del Bourgo and Catherine Bremer provided communications and publication support. Gabriella Scaduto-Mendola and Elizabeth Duckett dell'Osso ensured administrative support and formatted the document.

Table of contents

FIGURES

TABLES

Readers' guide

This is the fourth edition of *The Climate Action Monitor*, an annual publication by the OECD prepared under the International Programme for Action on Climate (IPAC). It provides insights on climate action by countries, building on the IPAC Dashboard of climate-related indicators, as well as other research and data from the OECD, the International Energy Agency, the International Transport Forum and the Nuclear Energy Agency.

IPAC reviews key trends and assesses progress in countries' climate policies, presenting key indicators in the IPAC Dashboard. In so doing, it complements and supports the climate change programmes across the OECD, such as Environmental Performance Reviews and Economic Surveys as well as the monitoring frameworks of the United Nations Framework Convention on Climate Change and the Paris Agreement.

IPAC focuses on developing country-level indicators for 50 countries and the EU. The countries covered under IPAC are presented in the Table below.

Table 1. IPAC country coverage

	38 OECD member countries	13 OECD partner countries
OECD Countries	Australia, Austria, Belgium, Canada, Chile, Colombia, Costa Rica, Czechia, Denmark, Estonia, Finland, France, Germany, Greece, Hungary, Iceland, Ireland, Israel, Italy, Japan, Korea, Latvia, Lithuania, Luxembourg, Mexico, Netherlands, New Zealand, Norway, Poland, Portugal, Slovak Republic, Slovenia, Spain, Sweden, Switzerland, Türkiye, United Kingdom, United States	
Key partner economies		People's Republic of China, India, Indonesia, and South Africa
Six accession candidate countries*		Argentina, Brazil, Bulgaria, Croatia, Peru, Romania, and (Thailand)*
Others		Saudi Arabia, Malta and the European Union

*Thailand became an accession country in 2024 but is not yet covered by IPAC data. While the Russian Federation is not covered by IPAC, the country is included in totals as part of IPAC's global monitoring effort.

This report presents data for countries covered under IPAC referred to collectively as OECD and OECD partner countries (which includes accession candidate countries, except Thailand), usually distinguishing explicitly between the two country groups. However, some indicators are not available for all countries and for all years covered. In such cases, the report either highlights these gaps in the text or provides estimates to ensure comprehensive aggregates are presented. IPAC estimates are preliminary, and work is under way on statistical methods to fill data gaps. For instance, data gaps for annual greenhouse gas emissions from OECD partner countries were estimated. Details on data availability and methodologies are provided in notes and the Annex.

The contents of the Monitor rely on a set of indicators developed with methodologies that have been declassified by members through the habitual OECD process and updated every year. To ensure that the monitoring effort is consistent and systematic, the structure of the Monitor, which is based on OECD Pressure-State-Response environmental indicator model (OECD, 2023[1]), remains consistent with slight variations in specific indicators or their visualisations to highlight an issue or trend that has emerged.

The main differences from the 2023 edition of the Monitor are that, in this 2024 edition the country coverage of GHG emissions and targets is global rather than just the countries covered by IPAC. These are consistent with the IPCC and the United Nations Environment Programme (UNEP) estimates (UNEP, 2024[2]). There are also some changes in the presentation of climate related-hazards data, showcasing maps for different regions. There are some new visualisations for section 3 to emphasise changing trends, and only data for country groups are presented. Finally, details of the methodology to estimate aggregate GHG emissions is presented in the Annex with a table with details on GHG emissions and targets. This year's results and new trends are reflected in the key messages of the Executive Summary.

Looking forward, IPAC will continue to construct extensive datasets for all covered countries and refine and develop indicators associated with this broader analytical perspective. In this way, it will help countries make informed decisions to address the climate emergency in the context of their country-tailored policy approaches, institutional landscapes, and economic and social realities.

References

OECD (2023), *The Climate Action Monitor 2023: Providing Information to Monitor Progress Towards Net-Zero*, OECD Publishing, Paris, https://doi.org/10.1787/60e338a2-en. [1]

UNEP (2024), *Emissions Gap Report 2024: No more hot air … please! With a massive gap between rhetoric and reality, countries draft new climate commitments*, https://www.unep.org/emissions-gap-report-2024. [2]

Executive summary

Climate hazards and disasters are increasing and devastating communities worldwide

The year 2024 is on track to set new records for global warming with unprecedented national temperature levels. For the twelfth consecutive month, the global average temperature was 1.5°C warmer than the pre-industrial era. By August 2024, 15 national temperature heat records were broken across the world. Increasing temperatures, coupled with increasingly variable precipitation patterns, have had dramatic effects across the world. For example, Southern Africa experienced its driest February in a century, while the United Kingdom experienced its second-wettest period in the past two centuries. The People's Republic of China witnessed a record number of significant floods, and the hottest July since 1961. Flooding in central Europe was unprecedented, a one in a 300-hundred-year event in terms of the extent of damages. Wildfires in Canada in 2024 have been devastating. These extreme weather events have destroyed lives and livelihoods with economic losses and damages yet to be fully assessed.

These dramatic events are confirmed by OECD data tracking climate-related hazards. Over 42% of the population in 50 countries and the EU covered under IPAC experienced at least 2 weeks of extreme temperatures in 2023. Of these, in 21 countries, the population exposed to tropical nights over 2019-23 increased by 10% compared to 1981-2010. The temperatures recorded in 2024 further highlight this trend, which not only has direct impacts but can also intensify hazards such as hurricanes, heatwaves, droughts and extreme rainfall. This, in turn, can affect vulnerable populations, ecosystems and infrastructure. Changing temperatures and precipitation patterns disproportionately affect vulnerable countries, exacerbating the impacts of extreme weather events and further deepening social and economic inequalities.

Agricultural drought conditions and extreme precipitation events are intensifying. OECD data on average soil moisture continues to fall in most countries over the period 2019-2023. These drought conditions can be particularly acute at the subnational level and during specific seasons, generating major social and economic consequences. This situation is aggravated by altered rainfall patterns. Over 18% of the population of countries covered under IPAC is exposed to the risk of river flooding. This risk can be as high as 40% for some countries. Similarly, more than 2.6% of the population in these countries is exposed to the risk of coastal flooding.

Triggering climate tipping points risks disrupting the climate on a global scale, creating a planetary emergency. Tipping points, such as the disintegration of ice sheets and the weakening of ocean currents, may already be underway and the risk of crossing more climate tipping points increases considerably at 1.5°C, potentially leading to catastrophic impacts on the climate. Meltwater from ice-sheet collapse, for example, contributes to a slowdown of the ocean currents, which in turn may contribute to impacts in other ecosystems, highlighting the interconnectedness of these major environmental changes. Immediate action to limit global warming to 1.5°C is essential to prevent cascading effects of climate tipping points that could lead to a planetary emergency.

GHG emission reduction commitments are not consistent with the Paris Agreement temperature goals. More ambition and efforts are needed to achieve net zero by 2050

The Paris Agreement has been crucial in strengthening climate action, but a significant ambition gap remains. By August 2024, 195 Parties have communicated their Nationally Determined Contributions (NDCs). However, emission reduction targets in the current set of NDCs are insufficient to achieve the Paris Agreement temperature goals. Even if current NDCs (considering unconditional targets) are fully implemented, estimated greenhouse gas (GHG) emissions are projected to reach 55 gigatonnes of carbon dioxide equivalents (Gt CO_2e) in 2030. This reveals an ambition gap of around 22 Gt CO_2e to limit global warming to 1.5°C estimated to be consistent with global GHG emissions of 33 Gt CO_2e.

Furthermore, the current net-zero targets are not ambitious enough. By August 2024, 110 Parties, covering 88% of global GHG emissions, have pledged net-zero targets. However, even if all these net-zero targets are met, total emissions are estimated to reach 21 Gt CO_2e in 2050. This will exceed considerably the 8 Gt CO_2e level estimated to be necessary to limit global warming to 1.5°C. In addition, the lack of legally binding net-zero targets in most countries poses a risk that these commitments may not be fully achieved. Only 27 countries and the European Union, representing 16% of global GHG emissions, have legally enshrined their net-zero targets.

Global emissions continued to grow in 2023. Global GHG emissions (including land-use, land-use change and forestry) increased by 1.3% between 2022 and 2023. This implies that current global emissions need to decrease by 2030 by 43% to achieve the 1.5°C and 27% to reach the 2°C temperature goals.

Given that countries are soon to submit the next round of NDCs for 2035 and Biennial Transparency Reports, it is critical that they address both the ambition and implementation gaps. Updated NDCs should be aligned with the 1.5°C considering economy-wide targets; and long-term legally binding GHG emission reduction targets will be critical for achieving the Paris Agreement goals.

Progress in national climate policy efforts remains insufficient. Policy implementation needs to be scaled-up.

The 2% expansion of government climate mitigation policy action in 2023 is not sufficient to meet countries' NDCs, indicating the existence of an implementation gap. The Climate Actions and Policies Measurement Framework (CAPMF) measures climate policy action by governments both in terms of policy density (i.e. the number of policies in place in a country) and stringency (i.e. the degree to which climate policies incentivise or enable GHG emissions mitigation). It is a climate mitigation policy database centred on a structured policy typology that tracks a common set of policies with harmonised policy attributes on an annual basis. It covers all OECD and partner countries except the USA. Over the last decade, climate policy action for the countries covered by the CAPMF expanded, on average, by 10% annually. However, in 2022 and 2023 climate policy action only expanded by 1% and 2% respectively. Although the CAPMF does not measure effectiveness directly, it is an indicator of policy effort. The observed slow expansion in climate policy action poses a risk of countries failing to achieve their NDCs. In fact, recent evidence from UNEP confirms that current climate policy action is not strong enough to realise the emission reduction targets set out in countries' NDCs.

The slow progress in climate policy action is underpinned by diverse policy developments across sectors and types of policy instruments. The expansion, albeit limited, was primarily driven by strengthening existing policies rather than by adopting new ones, highlighting the importance of recognising countries' efforts to increase policy stringency. Climate policy action concentrating on non-market-based policy instruments expanded thanks to strengthened regulations such as minimum energy performance standards. Policies related to setting targets, governance, the provision of climate data and international co-operation increased slightly after having grown significantly with the adoption of the Paris Agreement in 2015. However, policies implemented through market-based instruments declined, mainly due to reduced subsidies for renewable energy.

The gap in national climate policy action between OECD and partner countries continued to widen in 2023. While climate mitigation policy action expanded in both OECD and OECD partner countries, the gap in climate policy density and stringency between the two groups increased by 2%. Diverging climate policy action, especially stringency, affects competitiveness and may trigger carbon leakage, reinforcing the need for more international co-operation on climate policy action.

There is no one size fits all policy approach and no single recipe for their effectiveness. A policy mix results from a complex interaction between past climate action, climate ambitions, emissions profiles and available technologies as well as countries' cultural, social, political and institutional conditions.

Differences in climate policy action between OECD and partner countries is mostly driven by differences in policy density rather than policy stringency. OECD countries generally use more complex mix of policies to reduce emissions and strengthened their stringency. OECD partner countries have less stringent policies, though some countries reach stringency levels of OECD countries. The CAPMF data illustrates that some countries prefer to adopt relatively few, albeit stringent, policies. Conversely, others prefer to adopt many policies with rather low stringency.

Some sector-specific climate policy action has picked up in 2023. This was driven by increased policy action in the transport, building and industry sectors. In contrast, climate policy action in the electricity sector decreased, primarily due to fewer renewable energy auctions. The latter was accompanied by a rise of electricity-related emissions.

Climate policy action is misaligned with sectoral emissions profiles. Descriptive analysis from the CAPMF suggests that climate policy action may not be well-aligned across emission source sectors. For example, although transport accounts for the highest share of energy-related emissions in OECD countries, climate action is second to lowest. Similarly, in OECD partner countries, climate policy action in the electricity sector is the lowest, yet this sector accounts for the largest share of emissions. Although there are many other considerations, such as effectiveness, equity and costs, these, albeit indicative, results would suggest that there are possible avenues for more effective climate action by better aligning climate policy with emission sources.

To address climate-related hazards, countries are increasingly developing national adaptation strategies. There is significant progress in the number of countries submitting National Adaptation Plans (NAPs) and National Adaptation Communications to the United Nations Framework Convention on Climate Change (UNFCCC). However, it is still unclear whether these plans are underpinned by concrete policy actions and robust monitoring frameworks. More work is necessary to consistently track adaptation policies to support stakeholder engagement, promote peer learning and raise the efficacy of adaptation initiatives.

Looking ahead

Making progress towards the net-zero goals requires ambitious mitigation targets, effective implementation, and the adept navigation of the policy landscape. It is crucial for climate policies to be inclusive and aware of social and economic impacts, while remaining ambitious and effective. Countries must adapt their policies to ensure a just transition and protect vulnerable households and communities from being disproportionately affected. Understanding the full impact of these trends is essential for effective policymaking.

1 How far are countries from achieving national and global mitigation objectives?

The Paris Agreement has been instrumental in advancing global efforts to address climate change. The Agreement aims to limit global warming well below 2ºC by the end of the century and to "pursue efforts to limit temperature increase to 1.5°C" (UNFCCC, 2015[1]). To achieve this objective, countries or Parties to the Agreement commit to progressively reducing greenhouse gas (GHG) emissions through Nationally Determined Contributions (NDCs). As of August 2024, 195 Parties had communicated their NDCs with 110 Parties (109 countries and the European Union) pledging to achieve net-zero emissions, and 96 aiming for this target by 2050.

Current commitments are not ambitious enough to meet the Paris Agreement temperature goals. Global GHG emissions must be limited to 33 gigatonnes of carbon dioxide equivalent (Gt CO_2e) by 2030 to limit global warming to 1.5°C and 41 Gt CO_2e to limit global warming to 2°C. However, global emissions are projected to reach 57 Gt CO_2e by 2030 based on policies implemented as of 2024 (UNEP, 2024[2]). Moreover, even if countries fulfil their unconditional 2030 commitments, GHG emissions are estimated to increase to at least 55 Gt CO_2e in 2030. Similarly, global GHG emissions must be limited to 8 Gt CO_2e by 2050, yet the collective net-zero commitments would lead to at least 21 Gt CO_2e by that date.

Countries must increase their ambitions significantly and ensure the effectiveness of their policy effort. Estimates of GHG emissions indicate a potential average temperature rise of 1.7 to 1.9°C by the end of the century under the most optimistic scenario (UNEP, 2024[2]). Such a scenario assumes the full implementation of current NDCs and net-zero commitments for both unconditional and conditional pledges.

Global GHG emissions increased in 2022 and 2023

Preliminary estimates suggest that global GHG emissions (including LULUCF) increased by 1.3% between 2022 and 2023 (UNEP, 2024[2]). In 2022, global GHG emissions, including emissions from international aviation and maritime sources and land use, land-use change and forestry (LULUCF),[1] reached 55 Gt CO_2e. This represents a 0.3% increase from 2021 and a rise of around 9% compared to 2010.

Since their peak in 2005, GHG emissions in OECD countries have gradually declined, falling by 1.2% between 2021-22 and by 11% between 2010-22. They reached an estimated 13 Gt CO_2e in 2022. However, emissions from OECD partner countries have continued to rise, increasing by over 35% since 2010 and by 2% since 2021 (Figure 1.1).

Between 2021 and 2022, GHG emissions (including LULUCF) from major OECD emitters such as the United States, the European Union and Japan decreased by 1.7%, 2.5% and 2.1%, respectively, indicating a continued downward trend, although this was partially affected by the COVID-19 pandemic.[2] Similarly, large non-OECD countries, like Brazil and South Africa, experienced reductions in emissions by 0.9% and 3%, respectively. However, emissions increased in 22 countries during this period[3] with a concerning surge in large-emitting countries such as Indonesia and India, which experienced increases of 12.4% and 5.1%, respectively (IPAC Dashboard).

Figure 1.1. GHG emissions are stabilising in OECD countries while growing in G20 countries

Total emissions including LULUCF, selected country groups, Mt CO2e, 1990-2022

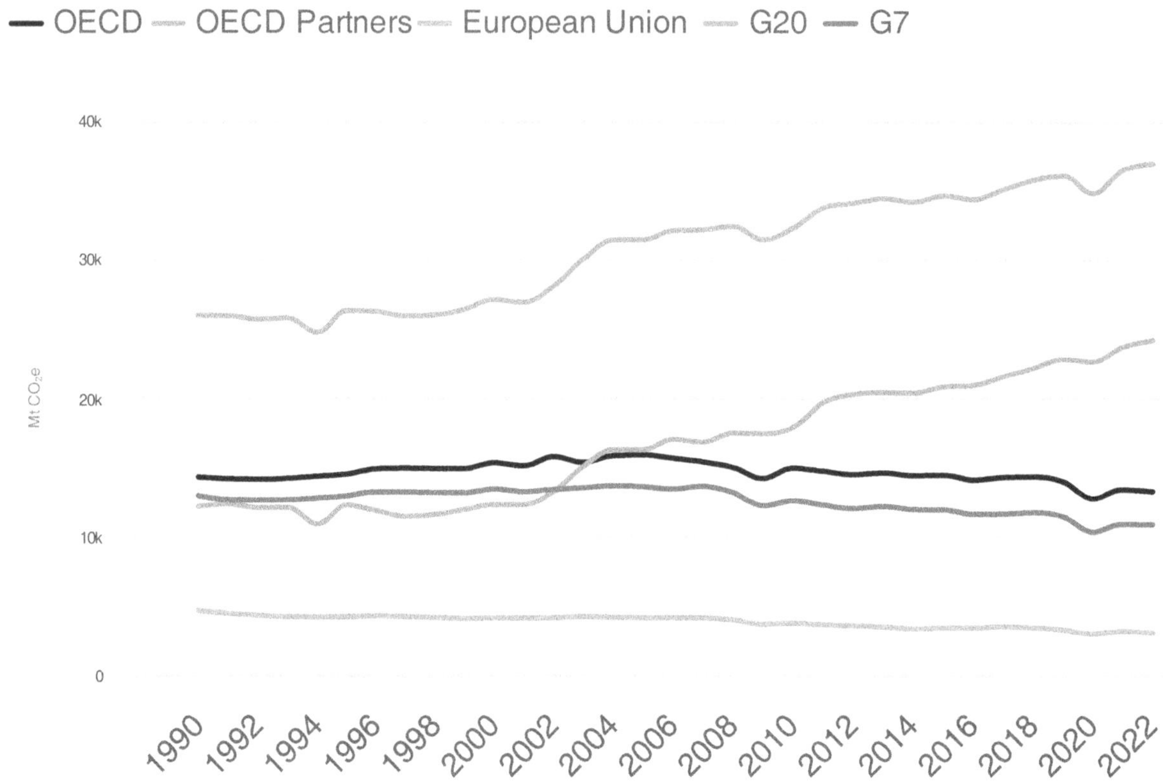

Source: Cardenas, M. et al. (forthcoming) "Greenhouse gas emission inventories. Filling the gaps in official data", *OECD Environment Working papers*, OECD Publishing, Paris.

GHG emission reduction commitments are not consistent with the Paris Agreement temperature goals

NDC targets are not ambitious enough

Ambitious mitigation commitments and their effective implementation are essential for meeting the Paris Agreement temperature goals. GHG emission pathways consistent with these goals would require reducing current emissions (55 Gt CO_2e) by at least 40% to limit global warming to 1.5 °C and by 36% to achieve the 2°C goal (Figure 1.2). Moreover, as recent estimates suggest, global GHG emissions rose by 1.3% between 2022 and 2023, which implies that current global emissions need to be decreased by a bigger extent by 2030 to achieve the 1.5 and 2°C temperature goals respectively (UNEP, 2024[2]).

In 2022, OECD and OECD partner countries covered by IPAC collectively accounted for around 80% of global GHG emissions, making their emission reductions a significant indicator of global climate policy action.[4] However, as of August 2024, the unconditional NDCs of OECD and OECD partner countries are projected to result in a reduction of just 4 Gt CO_2e by 2030 compared to 2022 levels. This represents an overall commitment to reduce aggregate emissions by 14% by 2030[5] with OECD countries aiming for a 29% reduction and OECD partner countries only a 5.7% reduction.[6]

These GHG emission targets set by OECD and partner countries are not ambitious enough to achieve the Paris Agreement temperature goals. Even if these targets are met, global GHG emissions are projected to remain around 55 Gt CO_2e in 2030, well above the 33 Gt CO_2e level required for 1.5°C and the 41 Gt CO_2e emissions necessary for the 2°C goal. This highlights the significant ambition gap between current commitments and the emission reductions necessary to achieve the Paris Agreement temperature goals.

Figure 1.2. NDC targets are not ambitious enough

Total emissions including LULUCF (1990-2022), NDC targets and IPCC estimated targets consistent with PA goals, OECD and non-OECD IPAC countries, Gt CO2e

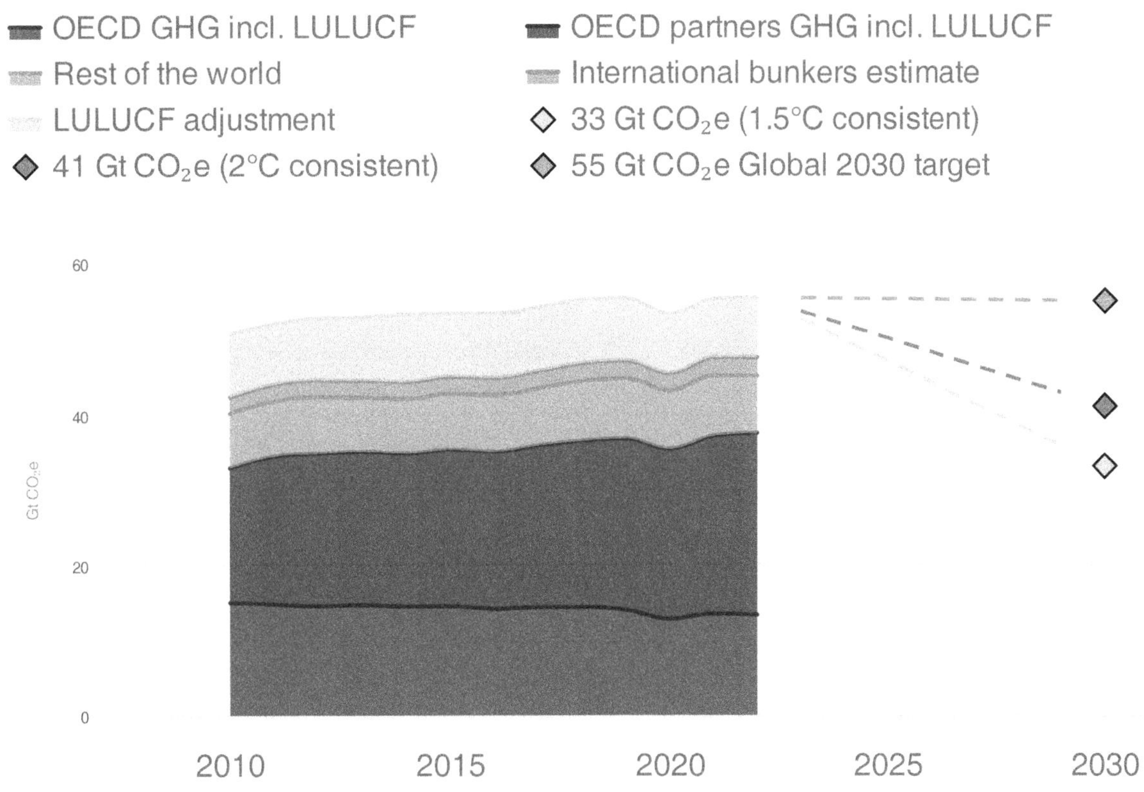

Note: LULUCF adjustment considers differences among the bookkeeping method as in (UNEP, 2023[3]) and national inventories.
Source : Cardenas, M. et al. (forthcoming) "Greenhouse gas emission inventories. Filling the gaps in official data.", *OECD Environment Working papers*, OECD Publishing, Paris; Pizarro, R., et al. (2024), "GHG Emission Trends and Targets (GETT): Harmonised quantification methodology and indicators", *OECD Environment Working Papers*, No. 230, OECD Publishing, Paris, https://doi.org/10.1787/decef216-en.

Net zero targets are not ambitious enough and most targets are not legally binding

An increasing number of countries are adopting net-zero targets for 2050 or later, with the count rising from 105 to 110 countries since last year. These commitments now represent 88% of global GHG emissions, up from 83%.[7]

However, estimated global GHG emissions even under full compliance with these net-zero targets indicate that total GHG emissions still fall short of aligning with the Paris Agreement temperature goals. Collectively, these commitments would result in global emissions of around 21 Gt CO_2e in 2050, significantly exceeding the required emissions of 8 Gt CO_2e to limit global warming to 1.5 °C and just above the emissions threshold for the 2°C goal (Figure 1.3 and Figure 1.4).

Figure 1.3. Current GHG emissions reduction targets have an ambition gap

GHG emission reduction targets are not consistent with Paris Agreement temperature goals

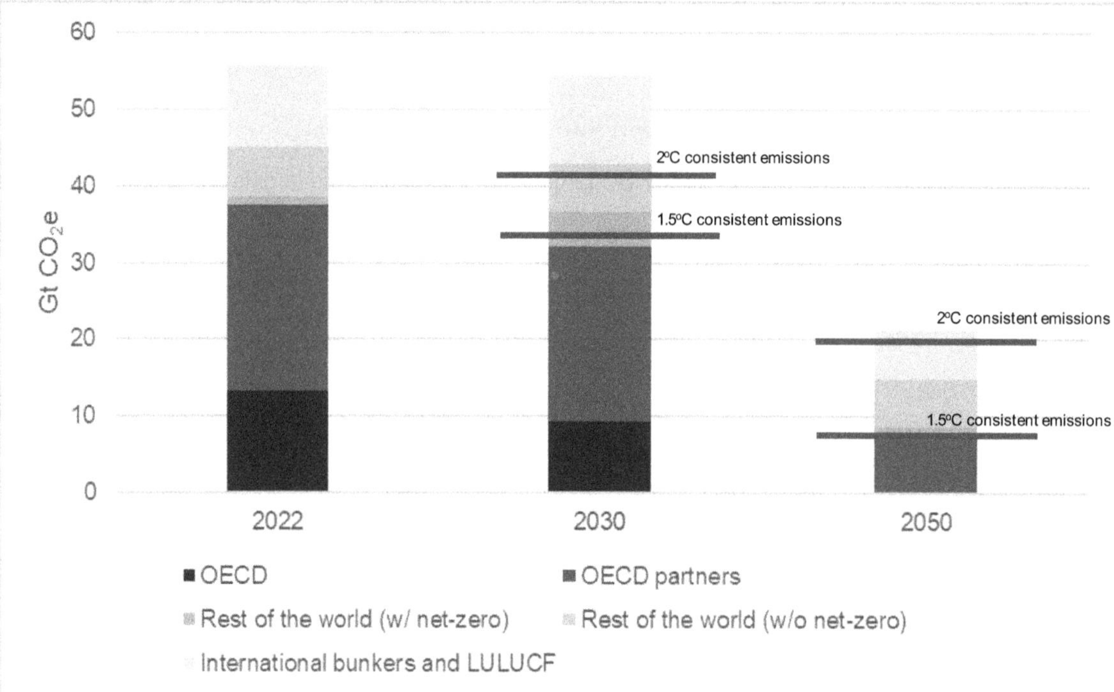

Note: "Rest of the world (w/o net-zero)" refers to the rest of the world emissions for countries that do not have a net zero pledge yet.
Source: See Annex for details of the methodology.

Moreover, the lack of legally binding net-zero targets in most countries poses a risk that these commitments may not be fully achieved. Only 27 countries and the EU (28 parties)[8], representing 16% of global GHG emissions, have enshrined their net-zero targets into legislation. The rest of the countries have pledged net-zero commitments through Long-Term Low Emissions Development Strategies (LT-LEDS), NDCs or declarations at high-level gatherings like the United Nations Framework Convention on Climate Change (UNFCCC) Conferences of the Parties (Figure 1.4).[9]

Figure 1.4. Only 27 Countries and the EU representing 16% of global GHG emissions have legally binding net-zero commitments

Number of countries with a net-zero pledge by type and their % share in global emissions

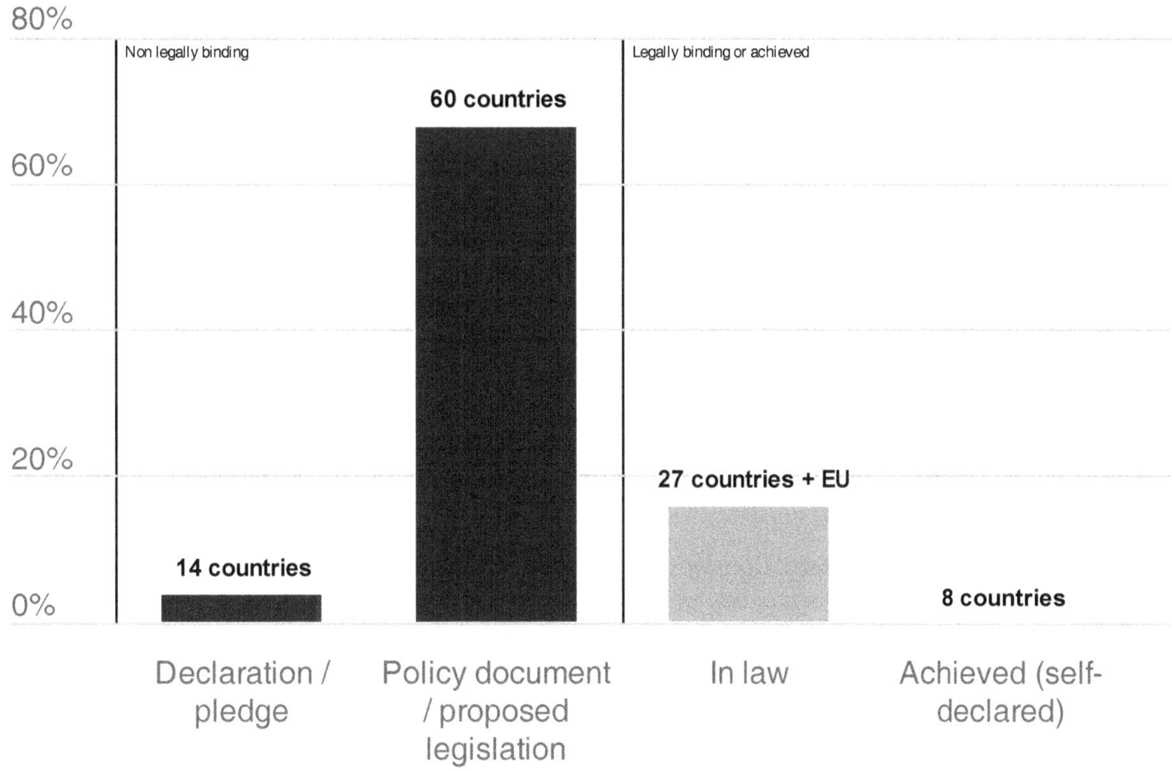

Note: Net-zero targets, climate neutrality, carbon neutrality and zero carbon are all considered as a net-zero pledge. The European Union commits to net zero by 2050 for the whole EU region. To avoid double counting, emissions for individual EU countries that have adopted net-zero commitments are not considered; they are covered by total EU emissions identified in the bar "in law".
Source: IPAC Net-Zero Tracker; OECD (2024), *IPAC Dashboard*, www.oecd.org/climate-action/ipac/dashboard.

Box 1.1. GHG emissions datasets at the OECD: Work in progress

The International Programme for Action on Climate (IPAC) provides foundational data and indicators to support countries' policy choices and contributes to several important components of OECD work on climate change. In addition to Net Zero+, for example, IPAC provides inputs to the Inclusive Forum on Carbon Mitigation Approaches and to Economic Surveys, among others. In so doing, it aims to develop a coherent and official estimate of greenhouse gas (GHG) emissions and targets. In this context, two working papers have been published (noted below) and a third is in review.

GHG Emission Trends and Targets (GETT): Harmonised quantification methodology and indicators (https://doi.org/10.1787/decef216-en). At the centre of the Paris Agreement are Nationally Determined Contributions (NDCs) that establish countries' plans to mitigate GHG emissions. However, NDCs differ across countries in terms of target types, coverage of sectors and gases. Developing countries may also distinguish between unconditional and conditional targets requiring international support. This makes it challenging to assess progress on mitigation commitments. This paper, published in March 2024, develops a methodology that harmonises countries' 2030 mitigation targets in physical units and provides clarity on sector and gas coverage. As such, it complements the efforts of the United Nations Framework Convention on Climate Change and facilitates the evaluation and monitoring of targets. The results are used to develop the GETT indicators for non-EU countries and the EU-27 covered under IPAC.

Greenhouse gas emissions data: Concepts and data availability (https://doi.org/10.1787/b3e6c074-en). GHG emissions data are essential for tracking progress towards the Paris Agreement's global temperature goals. In addition to the emissions inventories based on the Intergovernmental Panel on Climate Change guidelines, other GHG emissions datasets cater to different users and policy objectives. This paper explores the conceptual difference across approaches and presents and evaluates available OECD GHG emissions datasets. It pays special attention to coverage issues and data gaps. Finally, the paper outlines several steps to enhance data coverage and quality as part of a programme to develop a comprehensive and integrated GHG emissions dataset.

New momentum for net-zero pledges in international aviation and shipping

In 2022, a significant global sectoral advancement was the adoption of a net-zero carbon emissions target for international aviation by 2050, endorsed by the International Civil Aviation Organization (ICAO). The International Air and Transport Association (IATA) projects that about 10 billion passengers will fly in 2050, requiring a minimum abatement of 1.8 Gt CO_2 in that year. The collective abatement required between now and 2050 is estimated at 21.2 Gt CO_2 (IATA, 2021[3]). The key to ICAO's commitment lies in the development of the Carbon Offsetting and Reduction Scheme for International Aviation (CORSIA).

In 2023, member states of the International Maritime Organization also committed to reach net-zero emissions "by around 2050" for the international maritime sector (IMO, 2023[4]).[10] Together, the air and maritime sectors contribute to roughly 4-5% of global GHG emissions, with each accounting for 2% of global energy-related CO_2 emissions (IEA, 2023[5]).

GHG emissions are embedded in trade

GHG emissions embedded in trade play a significant role in the disparity of GHG emissions growth rates between OECD countries and partner countries. This discrepancy is linked to the outsourcing of carbon-intensive production to other countries, potentially leading to a global increase in GHG emissions. Such outsourcing can lead to carbon leakage, undermining environmental and climate policies if countries adopt less carbon-efficient techniques and less stringent environmental standards in manufacturing. Contrasting information on emissions based on both consumption and production helps identify the extent of this outsourcing.

Both consumption- and production-based emissions (excluding LULUCF) in OECD countries peaked in 2007 and have been declining. However, consumption-based emissions are considerably higher than production-based emissions in OECD countries. This disparity can be partially attributed to the imports of carbon-intensive goods from OECD partner countries (Figure 1.5). In contrast, production-based emissions are greater in these countries than ones based on consumption, and both have been continuously rising.

Figure 1.5. OECD countries drive GHG emissions in OECD partner countries through their demand for imported goods

Production- and demand-based GHG emissions, OECD and OECD partner countries, Mt CO2e, 1995-2020

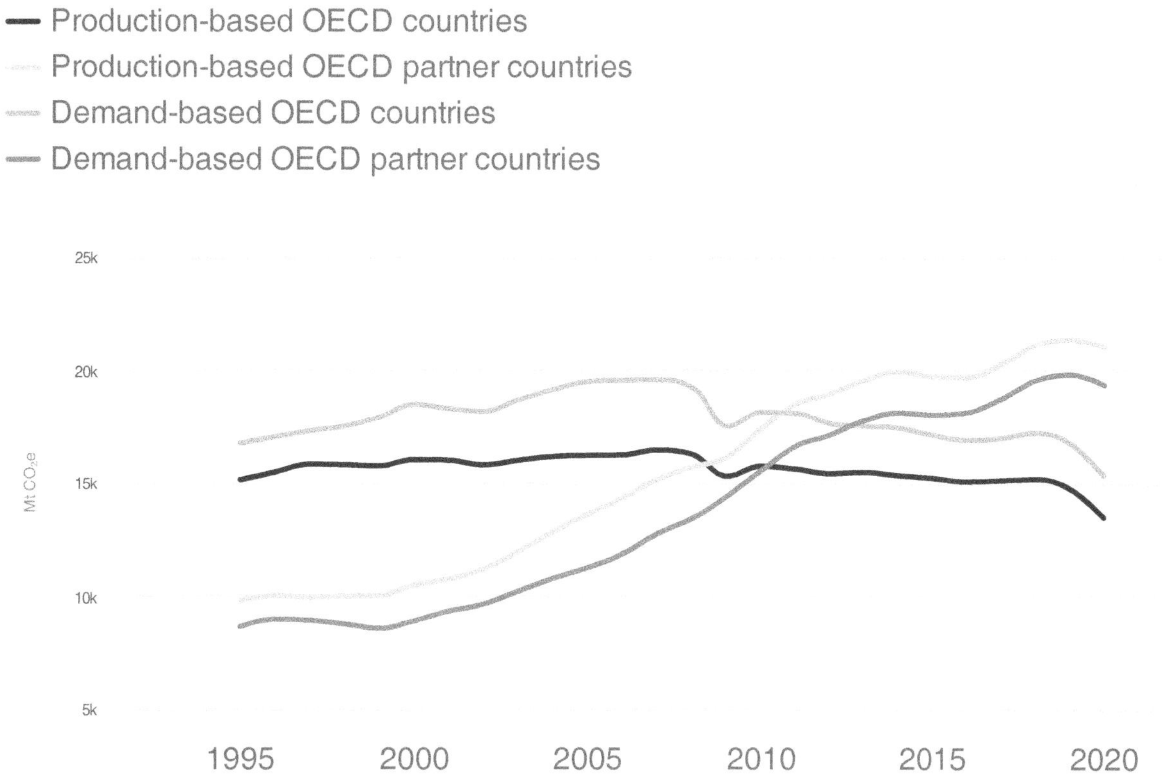

Definition: Production-based emissions are estimated according to the residence principle. They refer to the GHG emitted from the resident economic activities and households of a country. Demand-based emissions encompass GHG emissions from the resident households of a country, as well as direct and indirect upstream emissions from its final expenditure of final goods and services.
Source: OECD (2024), "Green growth", *OECD Environment Statistics* (database), https://doi.org/10.1787/data-00665-en.

Countries continue to decouple emissions from economic and population growth

Regardless of the sources for GHG emissions, the fundamental strategy for mitigation lies in decoupling emissions from economic and population growth. To measure the progress of decoupling, two complementary indicators compare intensity of countries' emissions: GHG emissions intensity per capita and GHG emissions intensity per unit of GDP.[11]

Per capita emissions have continued to decrease in OECD countries while increasing in OECD partner countries. Between 2010-22, OECD countries reduced emissions per capita from 11.8 tonnes to 9.6 tonnes.[12] Following a small uptake, mostly related to the recovery from the COVID-19 pandemic in 2021, this decline continued in 2022. However, although still lower than those of the OECD, per capita emissions in OECD partner countries have been steadily increasing since the early 2000s, reaching 6.2 tonnes per capita (Figure 1.6).

Figure 1.6. Emissions per capita have decreased in OECD countries while increasing in OECD partner countries

GHG per capita, OECD and OECD partner countries, T CO2e, 1990-2022

Source: Cardenas, M. et al. (forthcoming) "Greenhouse gas emission inventories. Filling the gaps in official data.", *OECD Environment Working papers*, OECD Publishing, Paris.

GHG emissions per unit of GDP have declined significantly since 1990 for both the OECD and OECD partner countries. In 2022, OECD countries continued this downward trend, while the decrease stalled in OECD partner countries. Although the pace of reduction was higher in OECD partner countries between 1990 and 2017, this trend changed from 2017. This, in turn, widened the disparity in emissions intensity between OECD and partner countries. By 2022, emissions intensity in OECD partner countries was still more than twice as high as it was in OECD countries (Figure 1.7).

Figure 1.7. GHG emissions intensity decreased in OECD countries, but stalled in OECD partner countries

GHG intensity per unit of GDP, OECD and OECD partner countries, T CO2e per 1000 USD, constant prices PPP, 1990-2022

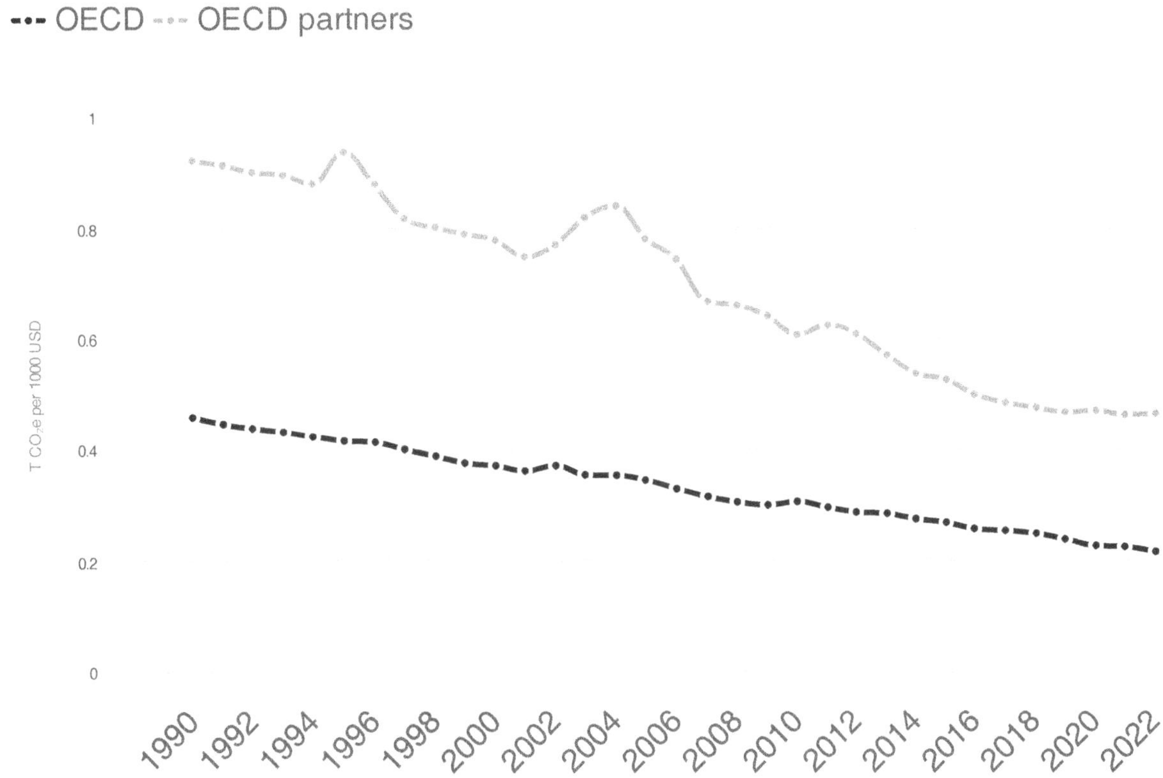

Note: GHG emissions are provided by PRIMAP and adjusted by the OECD. The last Climate Action Monitor used data from OECD (2023), "Air and climate: Air emissions – Greenhouse gas emissions inventories", *OECD Environment Statistics* (database), https://doi.org/10.1787/data-00594-en. GDP figures come from OECD (2024), "Green growth", *OECD Environment Statistics* (database), https://doi.org/10.1787/data-00665-en.
Source: Cardenas, M. et al (forthcoming), "Greenhouse gas emission inventories: Filling the gaps in official data", *OECD Environment Working Papers*, OECD Publishing, Paris.

The principal driver of GHG emissions is fossil fuel consumption

Emissions sources

Identifying emissions sources helps design targeted climate mitigation strategies (Chapter 3). These sources vary considerably across countries, depending on factors such as the level of development, natural conditions like weather patterns, available resources, distance to markets, economic sectors, energy resources and land use.

In general, the emissions profiles of OECD and OECD partner countries are similar. Energy contributes around 79% of emissions in OECD countries, with electricity/heat production and transport representing around 54% in 2022. In OECD partner countries, energy contributes around 74%, with electricity and manufacturing representing 54%. However, these total averages are influenced by the importance of China's GHG emissions in the manufacturing sector. Excluding China from the OECD partners group would imply that Energy contributes around 51% of emissions with electricity/heat production and transport representing around 41% and agriculture representing 15%.

Similarly, emissions from industrial processes represent 8% and 12% in OECD and OECD partner countries, respectively, while agriculture accounts for 10% for both country groups (Figure 1.8 and Figure 1.9). These aggregate percentages hide significant cross-country variation in emissions sources, suggesting the need for tailored policy approaches. The IPAC Dashboard shows country-specific information on these indicators. Carbon dioxide remains the predominant GHG in both OECD and OECD partner countries, accounting for 79% and 78% of emissions, respectively.

Figure 1.8. Most GHG emissions in OECD countries come from heat production and transportation

Emissions by sector, percentage, OECD countries, 2022

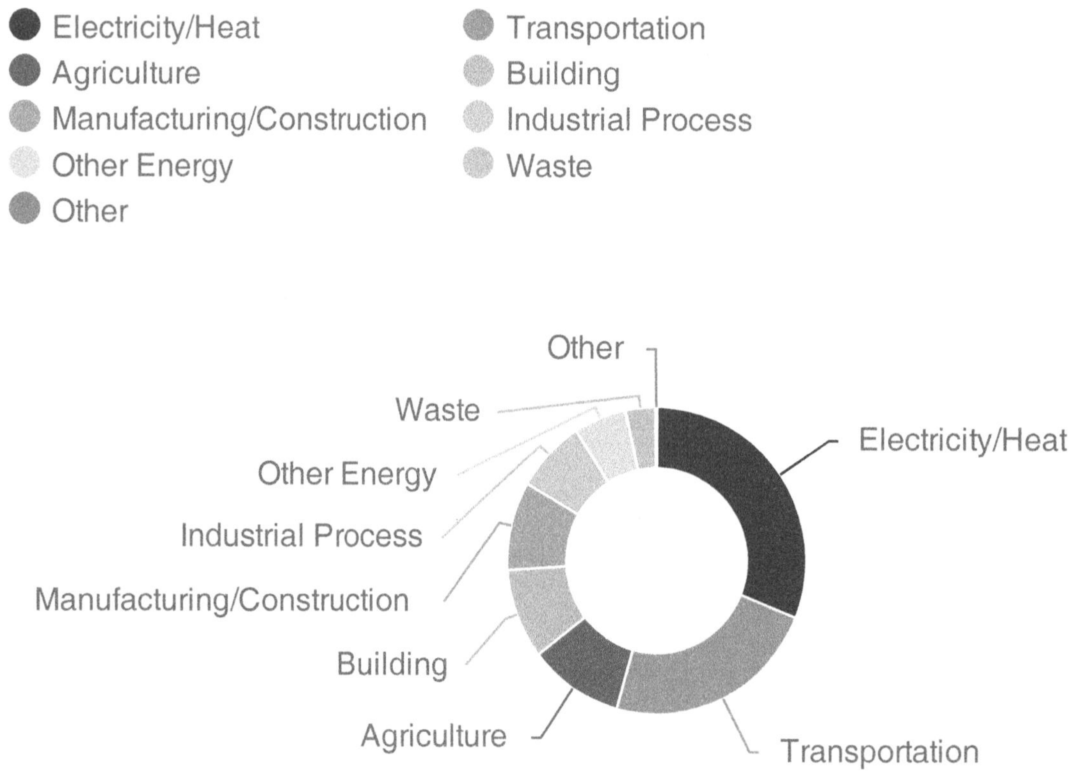

Note: IPCC's emissions sources classification categorises Electricity/Heat, Transportation, Manufacturing/Construction, Buildings and Other energy as part of "1. Energy". Climate Watch sectoral shares are used to disaggregate the energy category.
Source: WRI (2024), "Climate Watch Historical GHG Emissions"; Cardenas, M. et al (forthcoming), "Greenhouse gas emission inventories: Filling the gaps in official data", *OECD Environment Working Papers*, OECD Publishing, Paris.

Figure 1.9. Most GHG emissions in OECD partner countries come from the energy and manufacturing/construction sectors

Emissions by sector, percentage, OECD partner countries, 2022

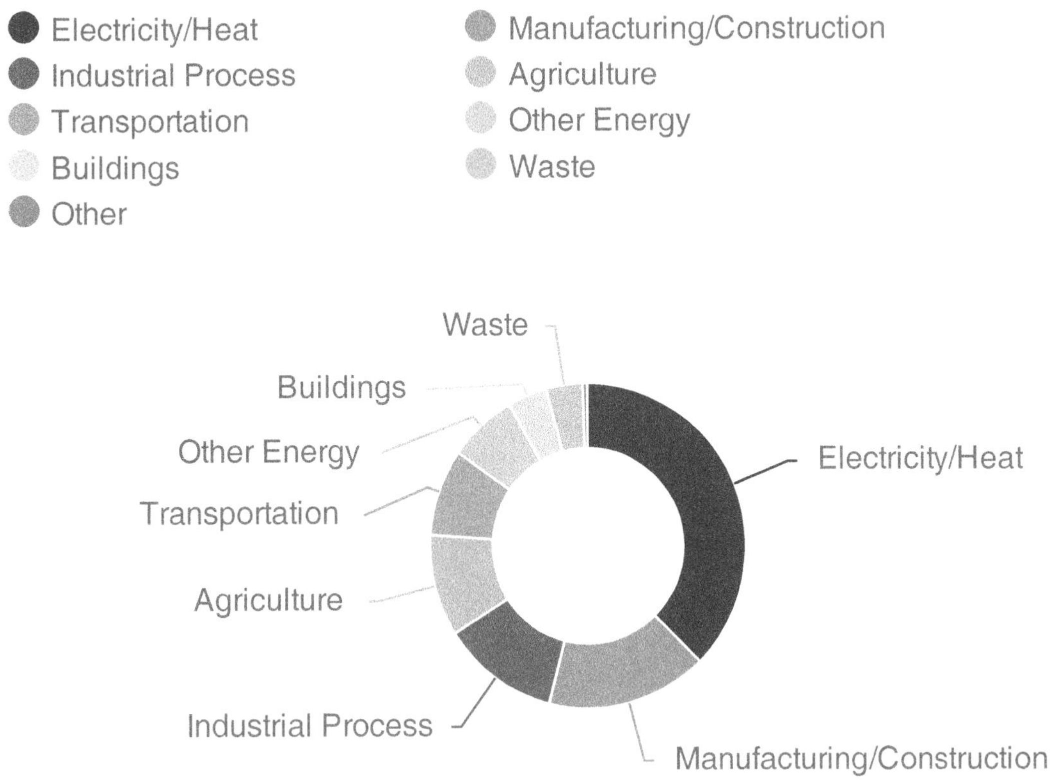

Note: IPCC's emissions sources classification categorises Electricity/Heat, Transportation, Manufacturing/Construction, Buildings and Other energy as part of "1. Energy". Climate Watch sectoral shares are used to disaggregate the energy category.
Source: WRI (2024), "Climate Watch Historical GHG Emissions"; Cardenas, M. et al (forthcoming), "Greenhouse gas emission inventories: Filling the gaps in official data", *OECD Environment Working Papers*, OECD Publishing, Paris.

Key drivers in emission source sectors

Although the reliance of the global energy supply on fossil fuels declined between 2012 and 2020, fossil fuel combustion remains the primary source of CO_2 emissions (Figure 1.10). Substantial investments in low-carbon energy sources and energy efficiency measures are critical to decarbonise the energy sector.

Figure 1.10. Reducing the reliance on fossil fuels is critical for climate mitigation

World share of fossil fuels in total energy supply, OECD and OECD partner countries, percentage, 1990-2022

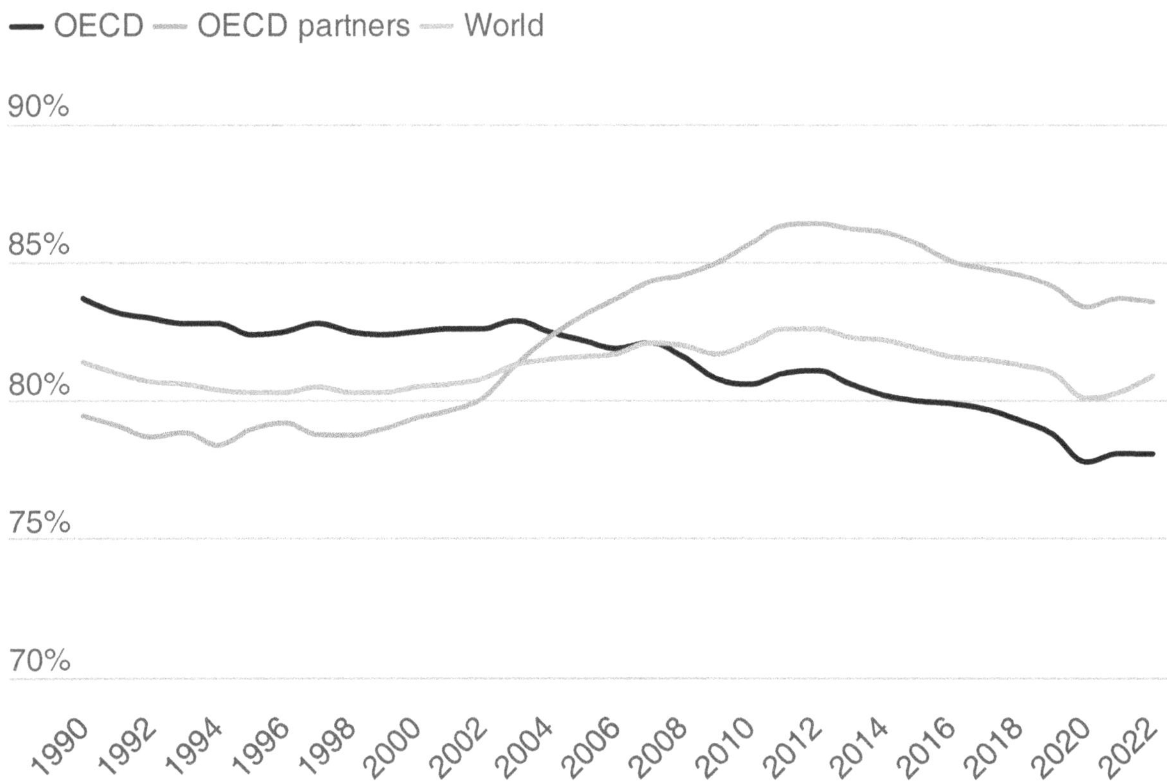

Source: OECD calculations based on IEA (2023), "World energy balances", IEA World Energy Statistics and Balances (database), https://doi.org/10.1787/data-00512-en.

In 2023, the deployment of renewable electricity continued its robust growth, yet it needs to further accelerate to reach the COP28 pledge of tripling renewable energy capacity by 2030. Decarbonising electricity production and electrifying end-uses represent key strategies for decarbonising the energy network. Most renewable electricity capacity added in 2023 stemmed from solar photovoltaic and wind sources. They experienced growth rates of 85% and 60%, respectively, jointly adding 540 GW of capacity (Figure 1.11). Despite this progress, countries need to ramp up deployment efforts to fulfil the COP28 pledge. While China and most OECD countries are making significant strides in renewables deployment, other countries are lagging (IEA, 2024[6]).

Figure 1.11. Renewable energy generation is growing

Renewable electricity generation, OECD and OECD partner countries, percentage, 1990-2023

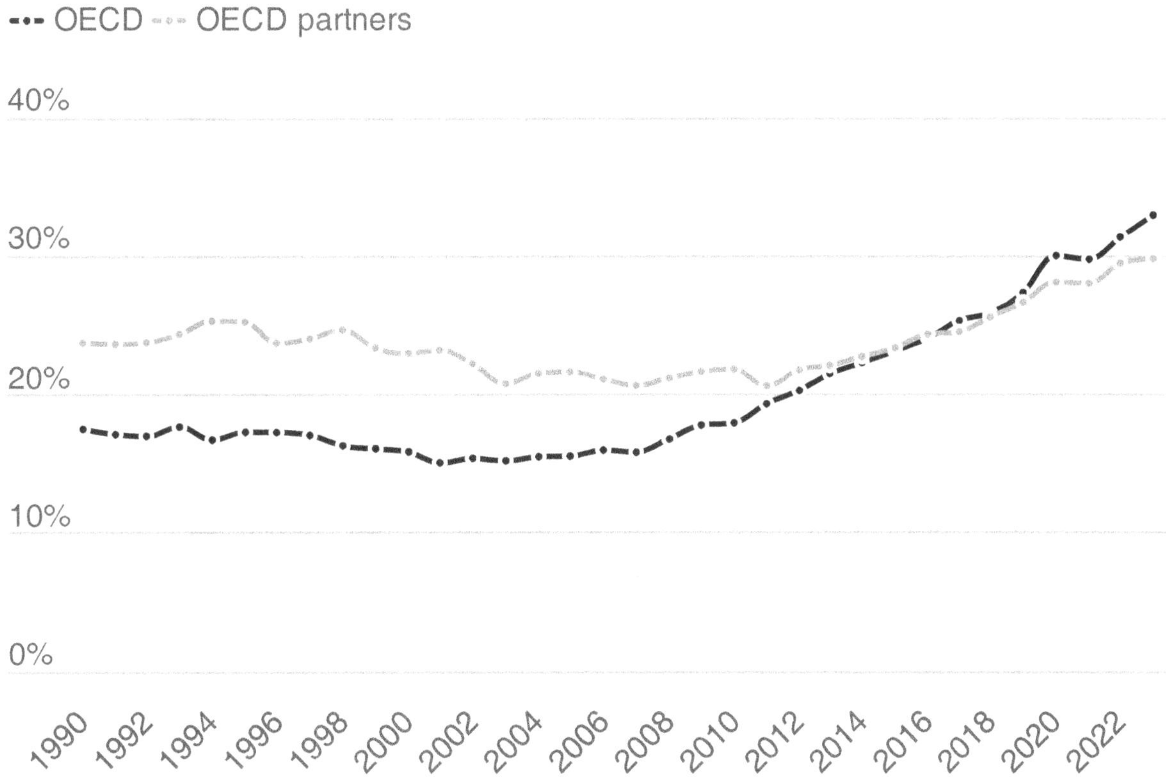

Source: OECD (2024), "Green growth", *OECD Environment Statistics* (database), https://doi.org/10.1787/data-00665-en.

Reducing emissions from the transport sector requires both reducing the number of passenger cars and switching from internal combustion engines vehicles to electric vehicles (EVs). Globally, sales of passenger cars remain high, with over 75 million units sold in 2023. Compared to 2022, EV sales grew by around 35% in 2023, reaching 14 million vehicles. This represents more than 18% of total passenger car sales in 2023, up from 14% in 2022 and 4% in 2020 sales (Figure 1.12).

Figure 1.12. Electric vehicle sales are rising rapidly

Global EV passenger cars sales and share of total passenger cars sales, 2010-2023

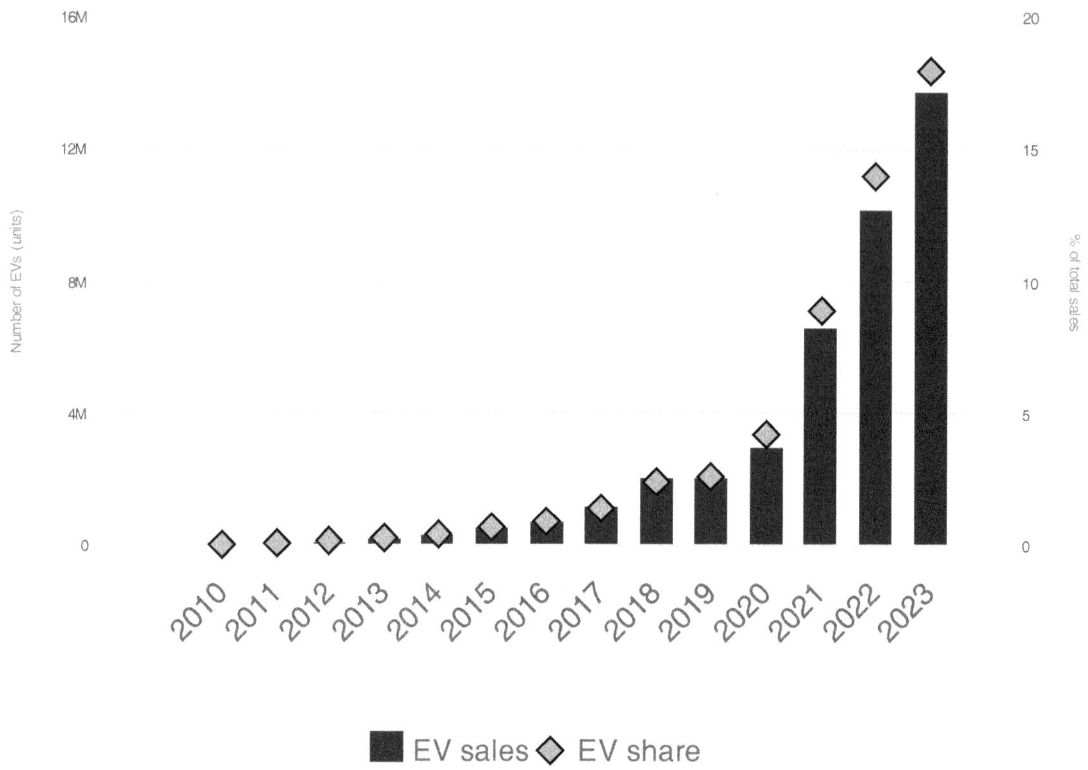

Source: IEA (2024), Global EV Outlook 2024, IEA, Paris, https://www.iea.org/reports/global-ev-outlook-2024.

Achieving net-zero targets and other environmental objectives such as biodiversity protection requires tackling deforestation, especially primary forests, in resource-rich countries. In 2023, 3.7 million hectares of primary forest were lost (Figure 1.13). Since 2002, total global primary forest has fallen by 6%.

Figure 1.13. Reducing deforestation is key to achieving Paris Agreement goals

Global primary forest loss (Mha) and 2001 primary forest extent remaining (%), 2002-2023

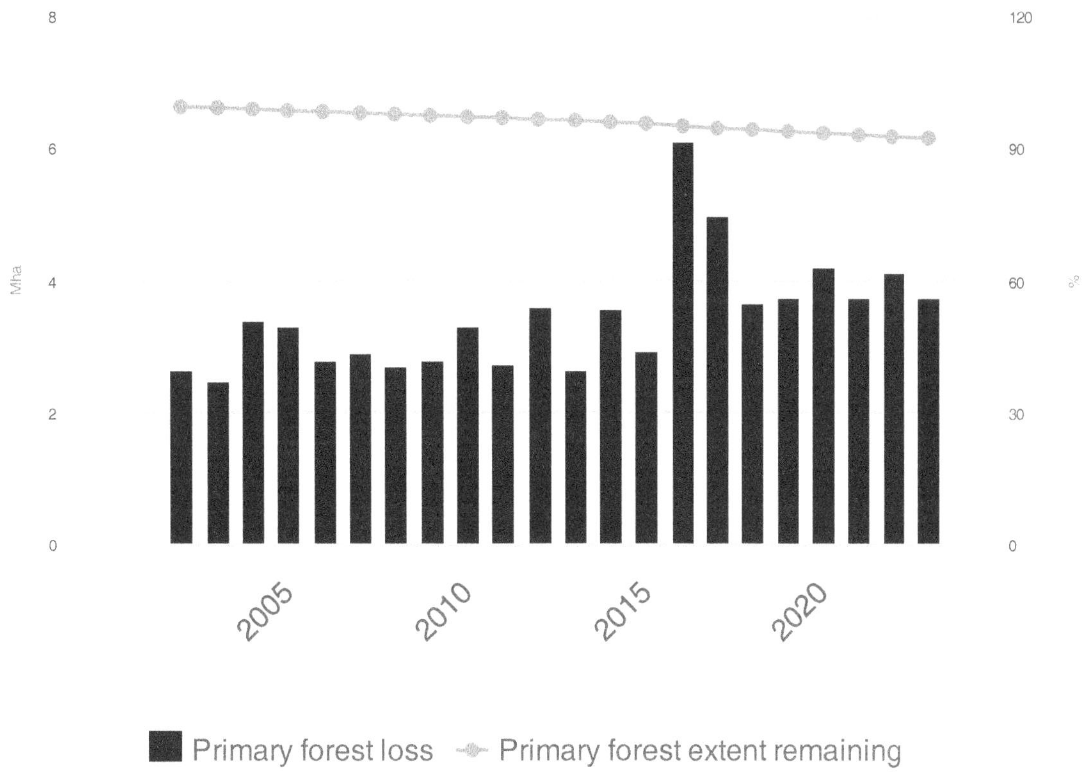

Note: Tree cover canopy density is set to >30%
Source: WRI (2024), Global Forest Watch, World Resources Institute, www.globalforestwatch.org.

Alongside energy combustion, deforestation remains a predominant global source of GHG emissions, albeit with a varied contribution across countries. Therefore, tailored policies will be essential to meet national mitigation objectives. This implies that countries do not necessarily need to prioritise the sectors that are major global drivers or uniformly reduce emissions across all sectors to achieve climate targets. Instead, policy choices should be consistent with countries' unique circumstances and capacities (IPAC Dashboard). As will be discussed in Chapter 3, there are general trends and common drivers, but no one-size-fits-all policy for all countries.

GHG emissions, economic growth and material use

Reducing GHG emissions by focusing on individual emissions sources is not sufficient because economic and population growth often outweigh efficiency gains and progress in decoupling emissions from production activities. In the long run, mitigating climate change and improving human welfare will rely on reducing material and energy demand across all sectors. Most OECD countries have managed to decouple GHG emissions from GDP growth. On average, GDP per capita increased by 57% from 1990 to 2022, while GHG emissions per capita fell by 26% in the same period. This progress can be attributed to the increasing decarbonisation of production with a ratio of GHG/GDP emissions (i.e. emissions intensity of the economy) declining to 0.4. Put another way, the production of a unit of GDP now generates four times fewer GHG emissions than in the 1990s (Figure 1.14).

Driven by China's economic success, OECD partner countries have experienced substantial GDP growth – over five times the growth registered since 1990. In the same period, GHG emissions per capita increased by only 42% while GHG emissions per unit of GDP fell to 0.3 (Figure 1.14). These impressive results indicate that economic growth and increased welfare can coexist with decreasing GHG emissions intensity. However, relying solely on further gains in energy efficiency will not be enough to put OECD partner countries on a path to net-zero targets. Advancing towards the energy transition is critical to achieve their mitigation objectives (OECD, 2023[7]).

Figure 1.14. Both OECD and partners countries have decoupled GDP from GHG emissions, but decoupling is slowing in OECD partner countries

GHG/GDP, OECD and OECD partner countries, 1990-2022

Note: GHG emissions are provided by PRIMAP and adjusted by the OECD. The last Climate Action Monitor used data from OECD (2023), "Air and climate: Air emissions – Greenhouse gas emissions inventories", *OECD Environment Statistics* (database), https://doi.org/10.1787/data-00594-en. GDP figures come from OECD (2024), "Green growth", *OECD Environment Statistics* (database), https://doi.org/10.1787/data-00665-en.

Source: Cardenas, M. et al (forthcoming), "Greenhouse gas emission inventories: Filling the gaps in official data", *OECD Environment Working Papers*, OECD Publishing, Paris; OECD (2024), "Green growth", *OECD Environment Statistics* (database), https://doi.org/10.1787/data-00665-en.

Material use must be addressed to reduce GHG emissions effectively. In 2022, total domestic material consumption reached 157 Gt, an increase of nearly 2% from 2021 and nearly 30% since 2010. Moreover, the extraction of materials is projected to surpass 111 Gt in 2030 and 167 Gt in 2060 (OECD, 2019[8]). To align with the goals of the Paris Agreement, it is essential to transition towards a more circular economy by reducing the material footprint: this is where GHG emissions are ultimately embedded (Figure 1.15).

Figure 1.15. OECD countries must reduce material consumption and increase circularity to reduce GHG emissions effectively

Domestic Material Consumption, IPAC countries and rest of the world, Gt CO2e, 2010-2022

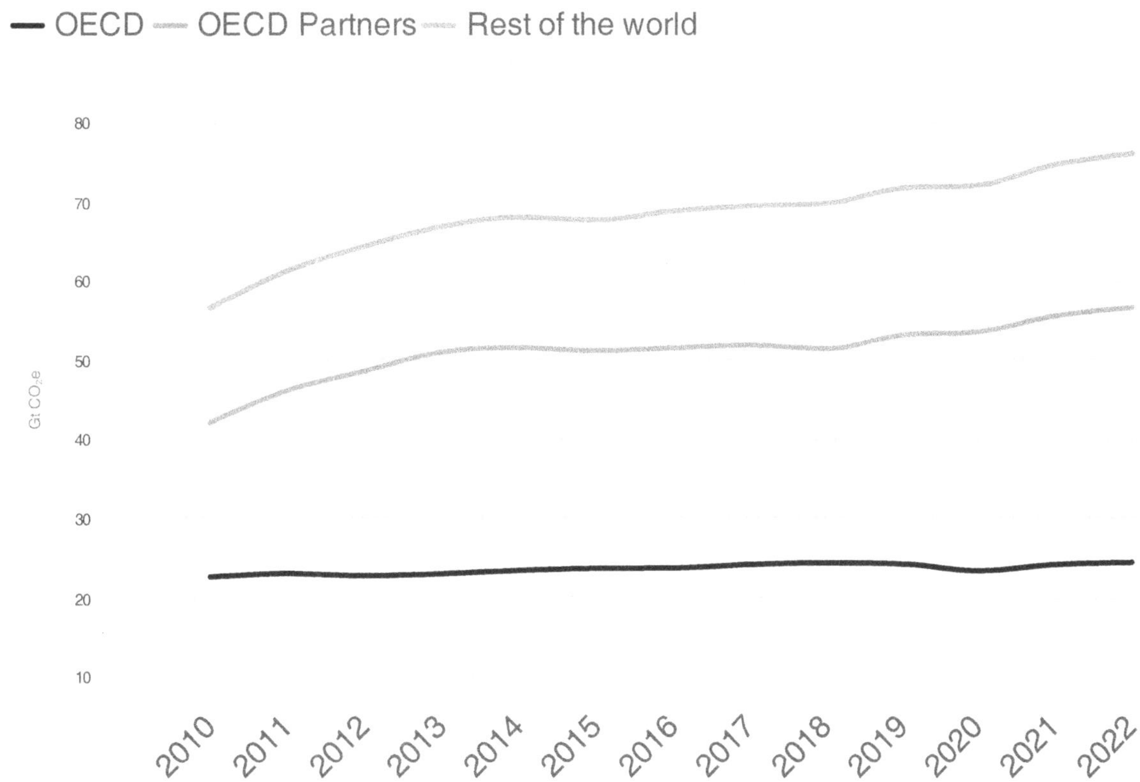

Source: OECD (2024), "Material resources: Material resources", *OECD Environment Statistics* (database), https://doi.org/10.1787/data-00695-en.

References

IATA (2021), "Net zero carbon emissions by 2050", Press Release, 4 October, International Air Transportation Association, Montreal, https://www.iata.org/en/pressroom/pressroom-archive/2021-releases/2021-10-04-03/. [3]

IEA (2024), *Clean Energy Market Monitor – March 2024*, IEA, Paris, https://www.iea.org/reports/clean-energy-market-monitor-march-2024. [6]

IEA (2023), *Tracking Clean Energy Progress 2023*, IEA, Paris, https://www.iea.org/reports/tracking-clean-energy-progress-2023. [5]

IMO (2023), "Revised GHG reduction strategy for global shipping adopted", Press Release, 7 July, International Maritime Organization, London, https://www.imo.org/en/MediaCentre/PressBriefings/pages/Revised-GHG-reduction-strategy-for-global-shipping-adopted-.aspx. [4]

OECD (2024), *IPAC Dashboard*, https://www.oecd.org/climate-action/ipac/dashboard. [9]

OECD (2023), "GHG emissions from fuel combustion (summary)", *Fuel Combustion Statistics: Greenhouse Gas Emissions from Energy*, (database), https://www.iea.org/data-and-statistics/data-tools/greenhouse-gas-emissions-from-energy-data-explorer (accessed on 1 August 2024). [7]

OECD (2019), *Global Material Resources Outlook to 2060: Economic Drivers and Environmental Consequences*, OECD Publishing, Paris, https://doi.org/10.1787/9789264307452-en. [8]

UNEP (2024), *Emissions Gap Report 2024: No more hot air … please! With a massive gap between rhetoric and reality, countries draft new climate commitments*, https://www.unep.org/emissions-gap-report-2024. [2]

UNEP (2023), *Emissions Gap Report 2023: Broken Record – Temperatures hit new highs, yet world fails to cut emissions (again)*, United Nations Environment Programme, https://doi.org/10.59117/20.500.11822/43922. [10]

UNFCCC (2015), *The Paris Agreement*, United Nations Framework Convention on Climate Change Secretariat, Geneva. [1]

Notes

[1] In this report, to present NDC targets including national LULUCF emissions, as is the usual convention, and be consistent with UNEP's total GHG emission estimates, we perform an adjustment consistent with (UNEP, 2023[10]), namely subtracting national LULUCF emissions and adding global LULUCF emissions. This adjustment reflects the different approaches taken by countries to estimate national LULUCF emissions from managed vis-à-vis unmanaged lands. To ensure consistency, UNEP estimates global emissions by aggregating GHG emissions from national inventories excluding LULUCF, and then adds a global estimate of GHG emissions from LULUCF for managed lands, this is referred to as a "bookkeeping" adjustment.

[2] Percentage changes are calculated using (OECD, 2024[9])

[3] Data are provided by PRIMAP and adjusted by the OECD.

[4] GHG emissions are estimated considering total aggregate country emissions including LULUCF, that is not including international bunkers and LULUCF bookkeeping estimates.

[5] GHG emissions inventories are compiled following territory- and production-based emissions principles. This means that, in most countries' cases, total GHG emissions does not include emissions from international transport. In addition, emissions from consumption of products produced in other territories or emissions from transporting these products are not included.

[6] In the IPAC Dashboard, GHG emissions targets are presented in scope defined by the countries' NDCs (including or excluding LULUCF, gases, AR) for aggregation; an adjustment was made to have a common scope considering all gases.

[7] Dominica, Georgia, Kenya, Micronesia and Mexico have been added to last year's count.

[8] Australia, Austria, Canada, Chile, Colombia, Denmark, EU (27), Fiji, Finland, France, Germany, Greece, Hungary, Iceland, Ireland, Japan, Korea, Liechtenstein, Luxembourg, Maldives, New Zealand, Nigeria, Norway, Portugal, Spain, Sweden, Switzerland and the United Kingdom.

[9] There are differences with other databases that also aim to identify the number of countries that have pledged net-zero targets. One of these is an IEA database, which presents differences with respect to some countries, in particular Brunei, Comoros, Cook Islands, Croatia, Ghana, Kuwait, Kyrgyzstan, Liechtenstein, Paraguay, Peru, Suriname, Tunisia, Tuvalu, Vanuatu, Vatican City (which IEA does not cover), and Mauritius and Morocco (which IPAC does not cover).

[10] Often countries' NDC targets do not cover international transport. Thus, these targets strengthen the commitments communicated through NDCs.

[11] Although focused on CO_2 emissions from energy, the former provides a measure of emissions intensity relative to total population; the latter, focusing on GHG emissions, provides a measure of the decarbonisation of the economy. Both measures provide insights into the relative emissions contribution of a country and its long-term emissions path.

[12] Data is based on adjusted data from PRIMAP, see Annex 1, differences in total emissions from last year's CAM2023 are related to different methodologies.

2 How are climate-related hazards and disasters affecting the world?

In 2024, the world once again witnessed the dramatic consequences of climate change – from record-high temperatures, storms and unprecedented rainfall to droughts, wildfires, and other intense and unexpected climate-related hazards. These impacts continue to pose serious threats to ecosystems and communities worldwide.

Extreme weather events are becoming the norm, leading to significant damages and loss of life. These effects can manifest as slow onset events (such as gradual sea-level rise) or sudden extreme events (such as flash floods or intense storms) (IPCC, 2022[1]). Between 2021 and 2023, annual economic losses due to climate-related disasters were estimated at USD 250-280 billion (Munich RE, 2024[2]; 2023[3]; 2022[4]),[1] while around 24 000 lives were lost globally as a result of these disasters (CRED, 2024[5]).

The dramatic extreme weather events changes observed in 2024 are isolated events but consistent with long-term trends that can only be understood by tracking hazards and disasters over decades. Drawing on global Earth Observation and other geospatial data sources, the International Programme for Action on Climate (IPAC) has developed indicators for a variety of climate-related hazards. The indicators focus on seven key climate hazards and four exposure domains, providing a time series that goes back as far as 44 years for all countries globally (Maes et al., 2022[6]).

This chapter explores the impacts and risks of climate change using historical observation data and introduces some key underlying data on future climate-related hazards. It shows how climate-related hazard exposures can vary across and within countries due to diverse geography, environment and weather patterns that affect each area in both OECD and OECD partner countries.

The indicators follow national and international guidelines and are based on the conceptualisation of climate risk of the Intergovernmental Panel on Climate Change (IPCC). These consider climate-related hazard, exposure and vulnerability as the key dimensions of disaster risk (IPCC, 2022[1]). The indicators have recently been updated and some key results are discussed below.

IPAC aims to further enhance this indicator set through forward-looking indicators for three key climate hazards and two exposure domains to 2100 (Box 2.1). Assessing future exposure of climate-related hazards is increasingly important. If the world continues on its emissions trajectory and does not meet the Paris Agreement temperature goals, estimates suggest that global gross domestic product (GDP) could fall by 7-10% by 2050 (Swiss Re, 2021[7]). If no action is taken, and temperatures continue to rise to 3.2°C by 2050, global GDP could drop even further – by 18% (Swiss Re, 2021[7]).

Box 2.1. Assessing future impacts and risks of climate-related hazards using IPCC Shared Socioeconomic Pathways

The Intergovernmental Panel on Climate Change (IPCC) uses and synthesises the scientific findings from climate models worldwide for its Assessment Reports. In work under development, IPAC uses the same projections from the latest generation of climate models that participated in the sixth phase of the Coupled Model Intercomparison Project (CMIP). The CMIP initiative serves as an experimental framework that harmonises climate modelling efforts across different research institutions worldwide. By using a multi-model perspective, it enables a more nuanced and reliable view of climate projections and captures the uncertainty inherent to climate models (Tebaldi and Knutti, 2007[8]).

Ongoing IPAC work uses CMIP6 Shared Socioeconomic Pathways (SSPs) that quantify and define the socio-economic circumstances - such as population growth, economic activity, energy intensity and land-use change - under which emissions, atmospheric concentrations and resulting radiative forcings can (or cannot) be changed (Riahi et al., 2017[9]).

Four climate scenarios are proposed (Figure 2.1Figure 2.1. Climate scenarios cover a broad range of CO2 emissions and economic development pathways). SSP1-1.9, the most optimistic scenario, represents a climate response to the Paris Agreement temperature goal to limit global average temperature rise to 1.5 °C by 2100. SSP1-2.6 also builds on sustainable development with substantial emissions cuts, but net-zero emissions are only reached after 2050.

SSP2-4.5 is a "middle-of-the-road" scenario. It offers differing levels of economic growth and sustainable development among countries that prevent reaching net-zero emissions by 2100. SSP3-7.0 presents a pathway where strong competition among countries and concerns over energy and food security hamper both mitigation and economic growth, causing emissions to roughly double by 2100.

Figure 2.1. Climate scenarios cover a broad range of CO2 emissions and economic development pathways

Global CO_2 emissions for CMIP6 climate scenarios

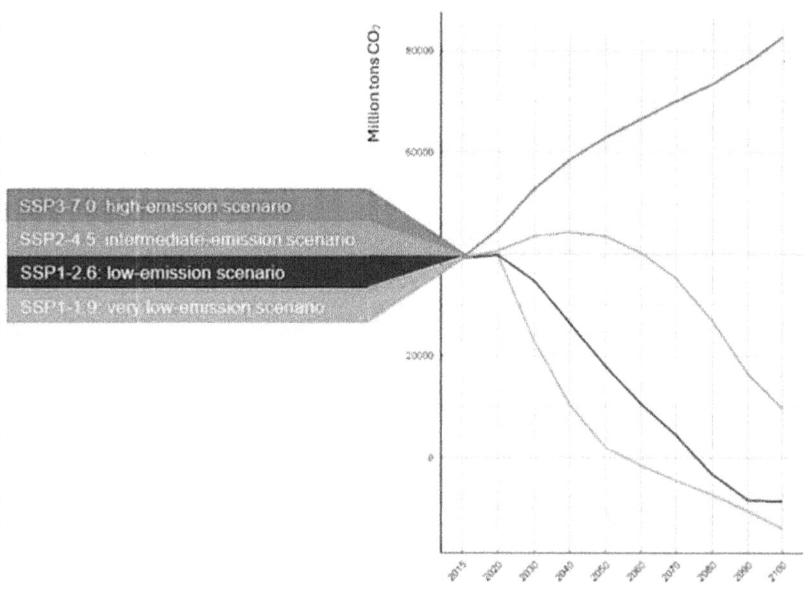

Note: This figure uses three Tier-1 SSP scenarios SSP1-2.6, SSP2-4.5 and SSP3-7.0 and one Tier-2 SSP scenario SSP1-1.9, while excluding SSP5-8.5 that is considered worse than the business-as-usual scenario.
Source: Data obtained from (Riahi et al., 2017[9]), (Rogelj et al., 2018[10]) and (Gidden et al., 2019[11]).

Rising extreme temperatures are affecting billions of people worldwide

Dangerous temperature levels are increasingly common around the world. IPAC data reveal a significant rise in the number of days with above-average temperatures across all countries (Figure 2.2. On average OECD and OECD partner countries experience an additional 30 days with above-average temperatures). On average, there were an additional 30 days per year with above-average temperatures across OECD and OECD partner countries in 2019-23 compared to 1981-2010. This corroborates recent findings that Earth experienced its warmest day in recent history with global average temperatures peaking at 17.16°C on 22 July 2024 (C3S, 2024[12]).

Figure 2.2. On average OECD and OECD partner countries experience an additional 30 days with above-average temperatures

Days with above-average temperatures, OECD and OECD partner countries, 2019-23 compared to the reference period 1981-2010

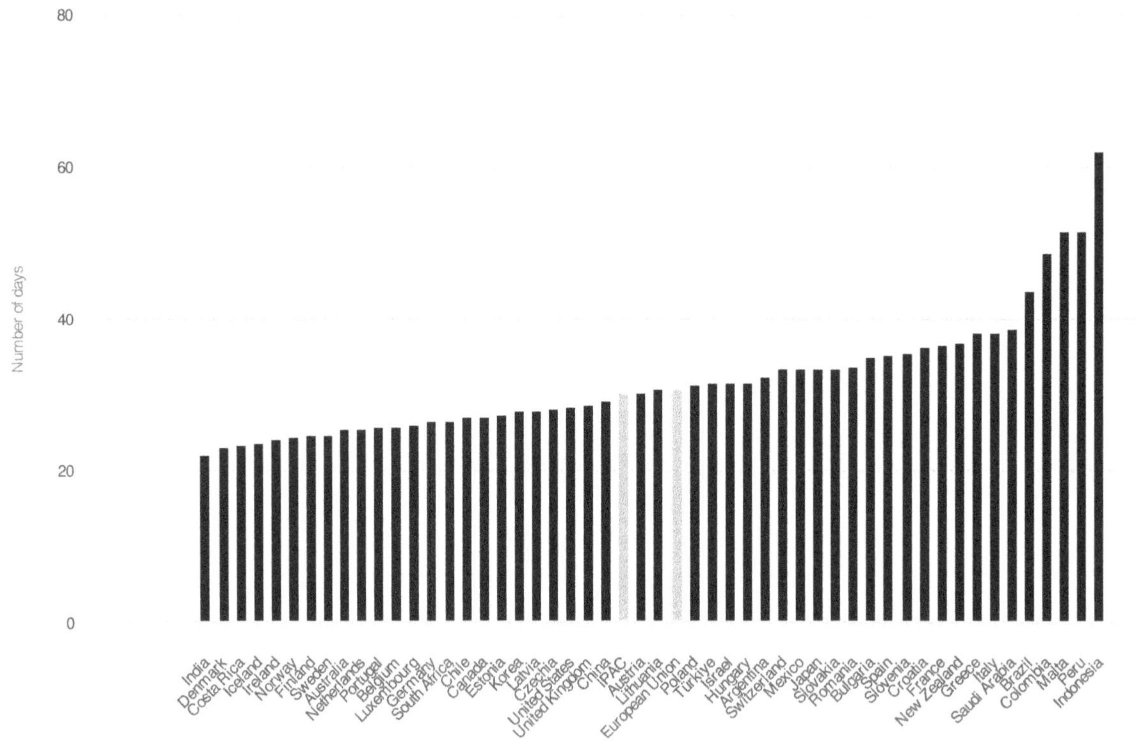

Note: IEA/OECD (2024), "Climate-related hazards: Expose to extreme temperature", *OECD Environment Statistics* (database), https://oe.cd/dx/58r.

Changes to extreme heat events involve determining a relative or absolute threshold beyond which conditions are considered extreme. In this analysis, which follows IPCC AR6 (IPCC, 2021[13])[2], a hot day exceeds 35°C (Maes et al., 2022[6]), while a tropical night does not go below 20°C. OECD indicators highlight that more and more people are increasingly exposed to extreme heat events. Since 1979, the population in all IPAC countries, both OECD and partner countries, has been increasingly exposed to hot days.[3] An estimated 12% more people in OECD and partner countries were exposed to such conditions in 2019-23 compared to the reference period 1981-2010 (Figure 2.3).

Figure 2.3. An additional 12% of the population in all IPAC countries was exposed to extreme heat between 1979 and 2023

Percentage of population exposed to more than 2 weeks of hot days, OECD and OECD partner countries' average, 1979-2023

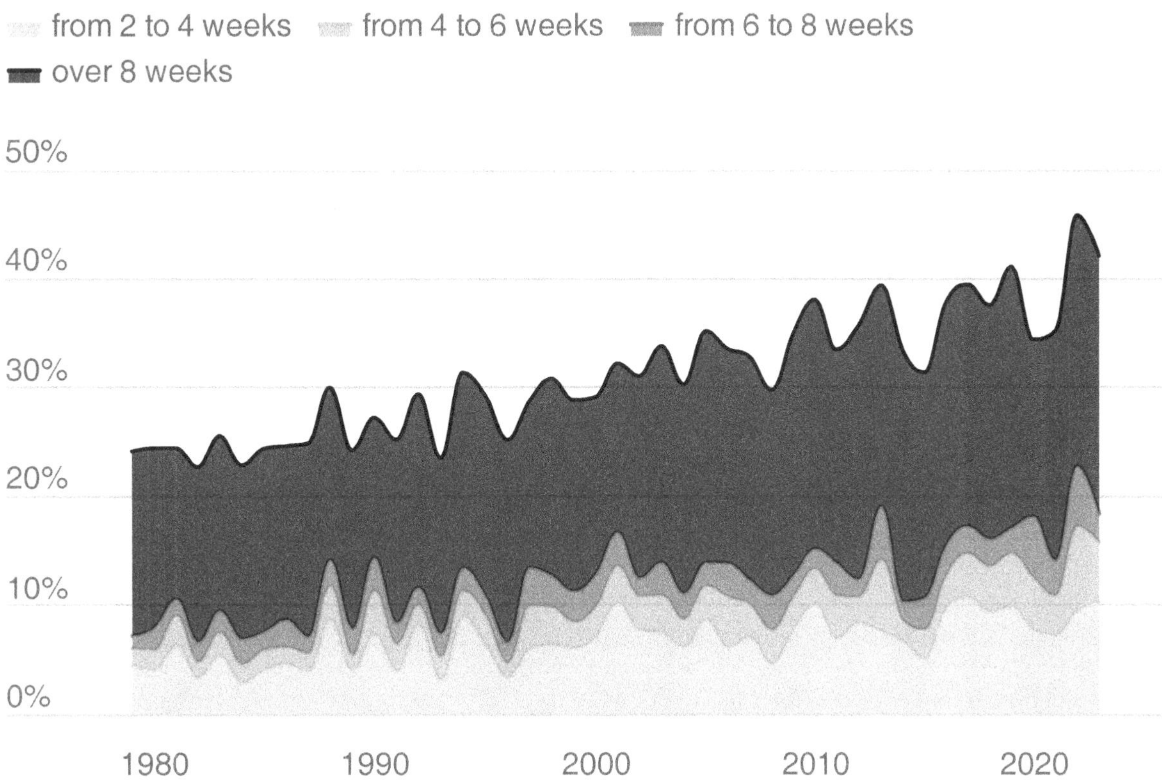

Note: Over- or under-estimations of the estimated exposure to extreme temperature are possible due to the spatial resolution of gridded data, particularly for smaller countries or regions. A variety of indicators has been developed that estimate exposure to extreme temperatures; these should be consulted for more detailed analysis of individual countries.
Source: IEA/OECD (2024), "Climate-related hazards: Exposure to extreme temperature", *OECD Environment Statistics* (database), https://oe.cd/dx/58r

Countries whose population was most exposed to hot days (more than 2 weeks) in 2019-23 comprise Saudi Arabia (96.5%), India (89.3%), Spain (35.4%) and Israel (32.4%), an estimated 1.5 billion people in total. Although historical exposure to extreme temperatures in countries such as Saudi Arabia and Israel was already notably high, exposure is lasting longer.

Reports on the ground corroborate OECD indicators, indicating 15 broken national heat records and an additional 130 monthly national temperature records shattered in the first half of 2024 (The Guardian, 2024[14]). For example, New Delhi experienced more than 40 days with temperatures above 40°C between May and June 2024, with one part of Delhi reaching 49.9°C. To make matters worse, hotter nights deprive people of the time needed to recover from the extreme heat experienced during the day. A report from the Centre for Science and Environment Analysis illustrates how heightened humidity and the urban heat island, driven by climate change, exacerbate heat stress conditions in Delhi (CSE, 2024[15]). Moreover, extreme heat is experienced differently across groups who do not have resources to protect themselves. Low-income people and environment systems are especially vulnerable to extreme heat (Page, 2024[16]).[4]

Climate scenarios also project that extreme heat will increasingly affect parts of Central and South America. Under a high-emissions scenario,[5] large parts of Central and South America are projected to face an escalating exposure to hot days by 2100, including countries such as Brazil, Colombia, El Salvador and Venezuela (Figure 2.4). This indicates that extreme heat exposure is likely to intensify, even in tropical areas that traditionally encounter high levels of extreme heat during certain times of the year.

Figure 2.4. By 2100, extreme heat is projected to intensify in parts of Central and South America

Additional yearly number of hot days under a high-emissions scenario, Central and South America, 2080-2099, compared to the reference period 1995-2014.

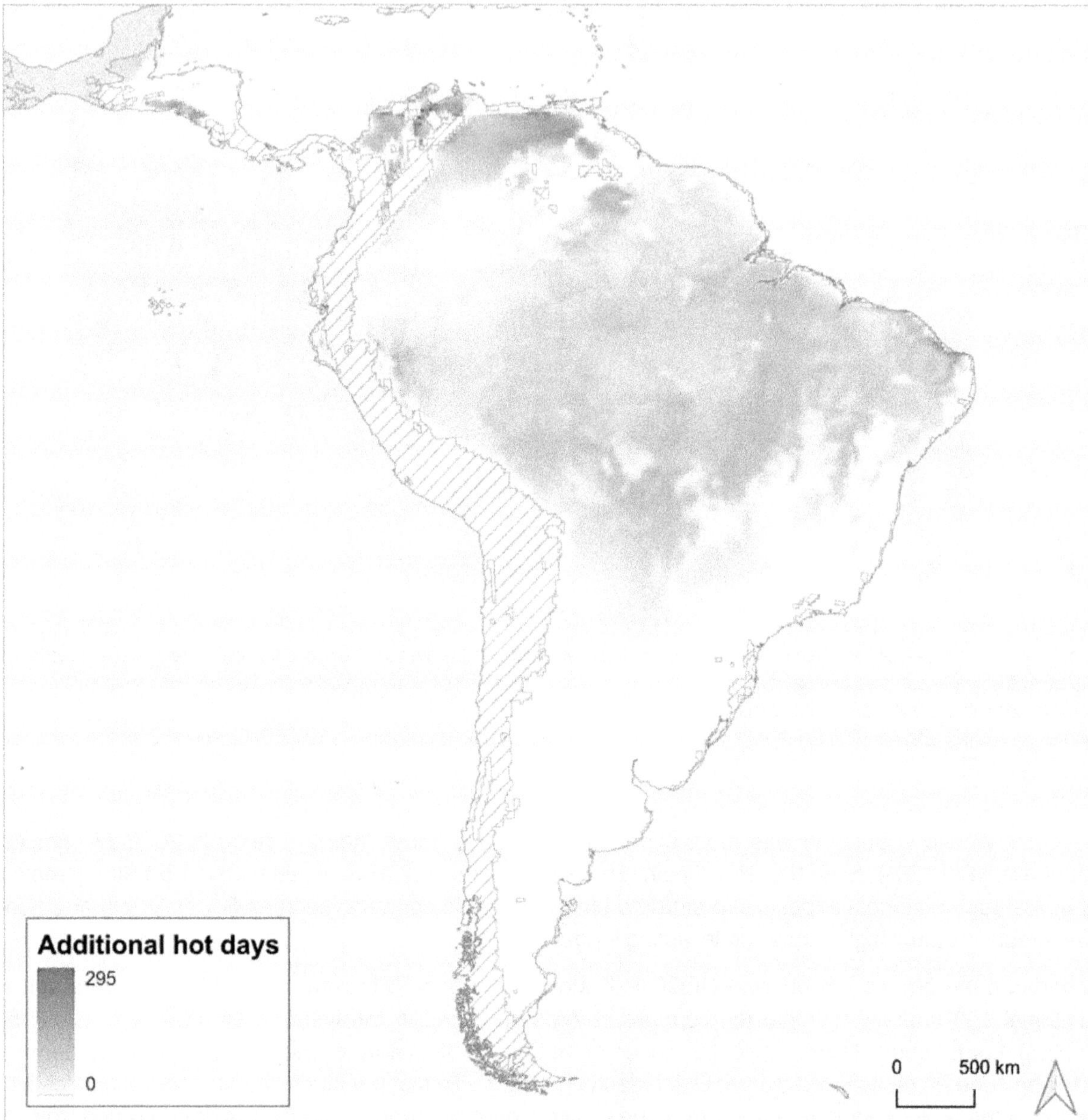

Note: More information on a high-emissions scenario can be found in Box 2.1. No robust change is illustrated as dashed area.
Robust change of values in a multi-model ensemble are defined as where ≥ 66% of climate models show a significant change (i.e. change greater than the variability threshold) and where ≥ 80% of all climate models agree on the sign of change (IPCC, 2021[13]).
Source: OECD visualisation using data from (Climate Change Knowledge Portal, 2024[17]).

Tropical nights, associated with high night-time temperatures, generate risks to human health due to sleep disturbances and inability to cool down at night (Seltenrich, 2023[18]), as well as increased economic costs. In the 44 years between 1979-83 and 2019-23, OECD and partner countries experienced an estimated increase in nine additional tropical nights. Of the 50 countries and the EU covered, 21 had more than an additional 10% of their population exposed to tropical nights[6] over 2019-23 compared to 1981-2010. Meanwhile, countries such as Korea (28.9%), Italy (19.6%) and Greece (17%) had the highest increase in population exposed to more than 8 weeks of tropical nights[7] (Figure 2.5).

Figure 2.5. On average there are over 9 extra tropical nights a year over a period of 44 years

Percentage of population exposed to more than 2 weeks of tropical nights, OECD and OECD partner countries, 2019-23 average

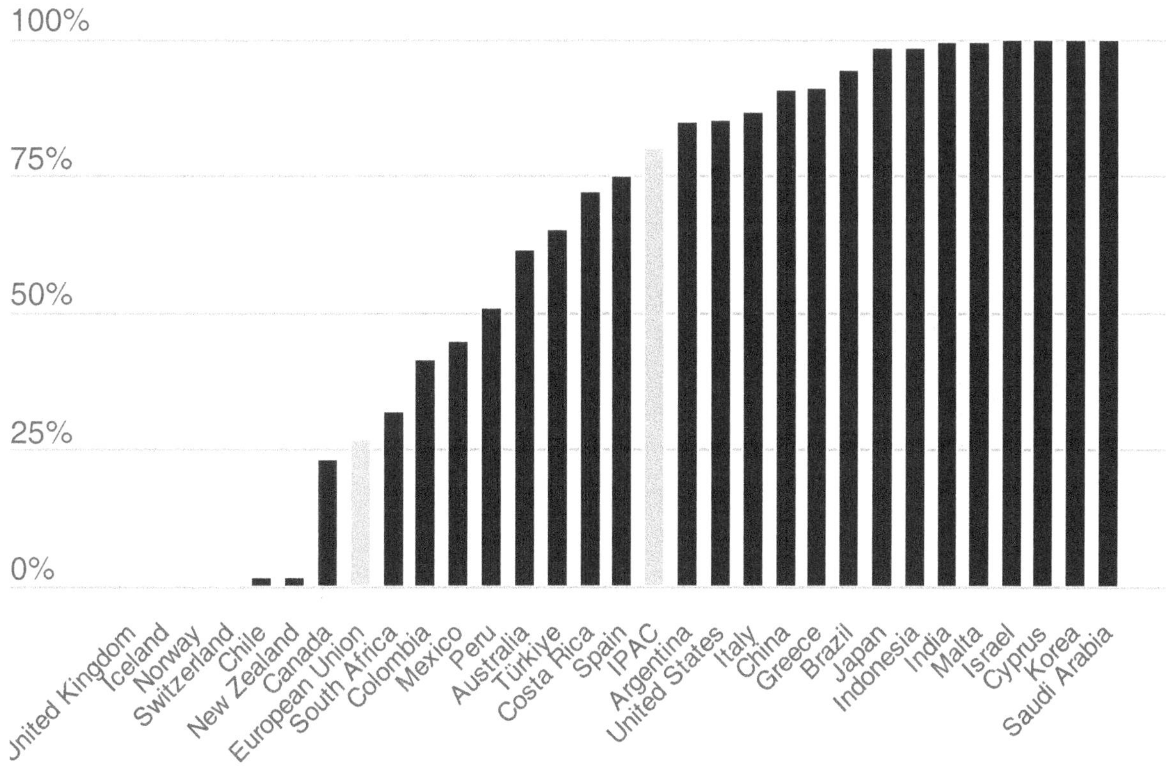

Note: Over- or under-estimations of the estimated exposure to extreme temperature are possible due to the spatial resolution of gridded data, particularly for smaller countries or regions. A variety of indicators has been developed that estimate exposure to extreme temperatures; these should be consulted for more detailed analysis of individual countries.

Source: IEA/OECD (2024), "Climate-related hazards: Exposure to extreme temperature", *OECD Environment Statistics* (database), https://oe.cd/dx/58r

In line with the increasing average temperature trend, the exposure to extreme cold is decreasing. The share of global population exposed to icing days is decreasing year by year. An estimated 6.9% fewer people faced such conditions during 2019-23 compared to 1981-2010.

Worsening droughts threaten food supplies

Rising temperatures have adverse effects on food systems, with croplands increasingly more vulnerable to agricultural droughts. Across the OECD and OECD partner countries, there was a significant decrease in soil moisture levels on croplands (2.9%) during 2019-23 compared to the reference period 1981-2010. The countries most affected by agricultural droughts include Argentina, Brazil, Mexico, and Romania, that witnessed average declines exceeding 6% in cropland soil moisture over the past five years (Figure 2.6). In fact, Argentina, Brazil and Mexico recorded their highest decline in cropland soil moisture in 2023 since the starting period of this indicator (1981).

Figure 2.6. In 2023, agricultural drought worsened with a 2.9% decrease in cropland soil moisture

Cropland soil moisture anomaly (%), 2019-23 average compared to the reference period 1981-2010

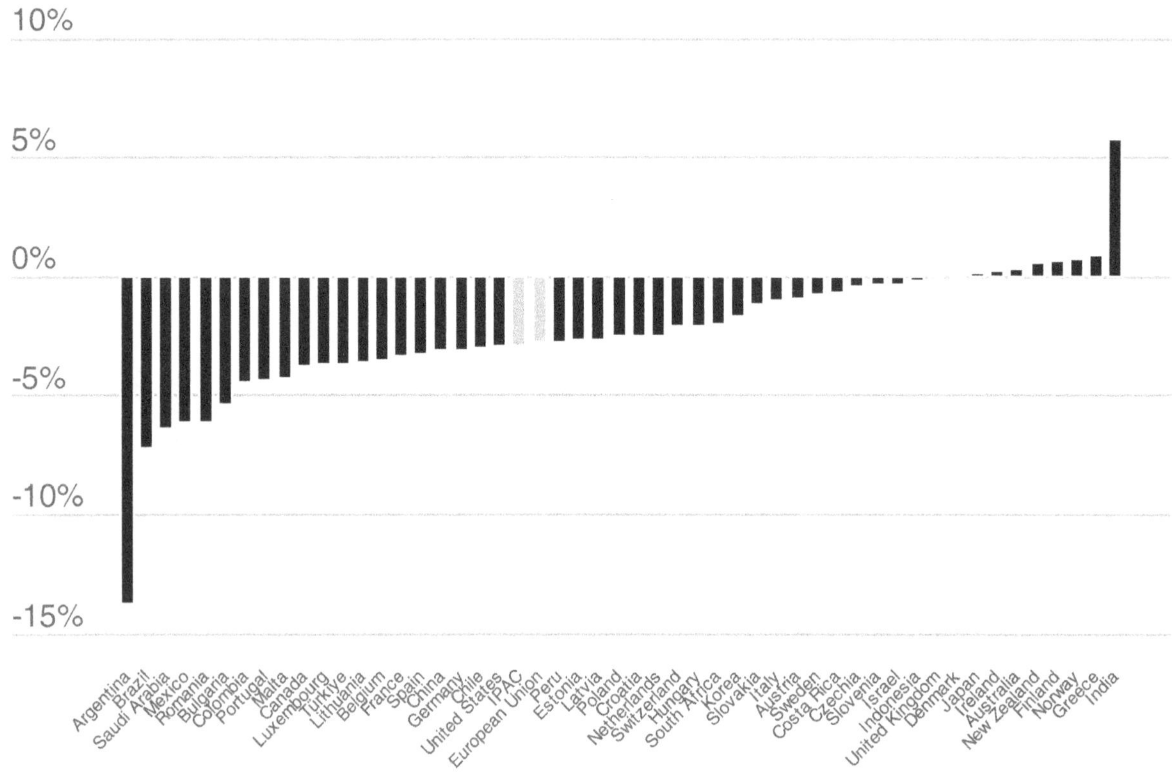

Note: No results are available for Iceland since no cropland cover is detected using Copernicus global land cover data. Caution is advised interpreting results for Saudi Arabia because cropland cover is low.
Source: IEA/OECD (2024), "Climate-related hazards: Exposure to drought", *OECD Environment Statistics* (database), https://oe.cd/dx/58t

National averages hide large differences and changes at the subnational level, where recorded drops in soil moisture are greater (Figure 2.7). In Europe, for example, OECD data show that South East, North East and South Muntenia in Romania have experienced severe soil moisture declines of 9.2%, 8.5% and 7.2%, respectively (Figure 2.7). Similarly, the Bulgarian regions of North East, North Central and South East experienced soil moisture declines of 8%, 7.6% and 5.4%, respectively.

These findings are concerning, especially since these regions have more than 50% cropland cover, and since agriculture plays an important socio-economic role in people's lives and livelihoods. Most of Romania's poor live in rural areas, for example, and depend on agriculture-related activities for their livelihoods (World Bank, 2018[19]). As 2024 unfolded, Romanian farmers faced another difficult year due to lack of rain.

Worsening drought conditions in these regions underscore a grim reality: climate change is intensifying the frequency and severity of such impacts. With each passing year, the effects of climate change are becoming more pronounced. Already, fragile agricultural sectors in regions of Romania, Bulgaria and elsewhere are increasingly at risk. Dwindling soil moisture makes it harder to sustain crops and, by extension, livelihoods. Substantial efforts are needed to address the root causes of climate change and build resilience in these vulnerable areas.

Figure 2.7. Regions in southern and eastern Europe are experiencing the most severe drought impacts in Europe

Land soil moisture anomaly (%), 2019-23 average compared to the reference period 1981-2010 across Europe

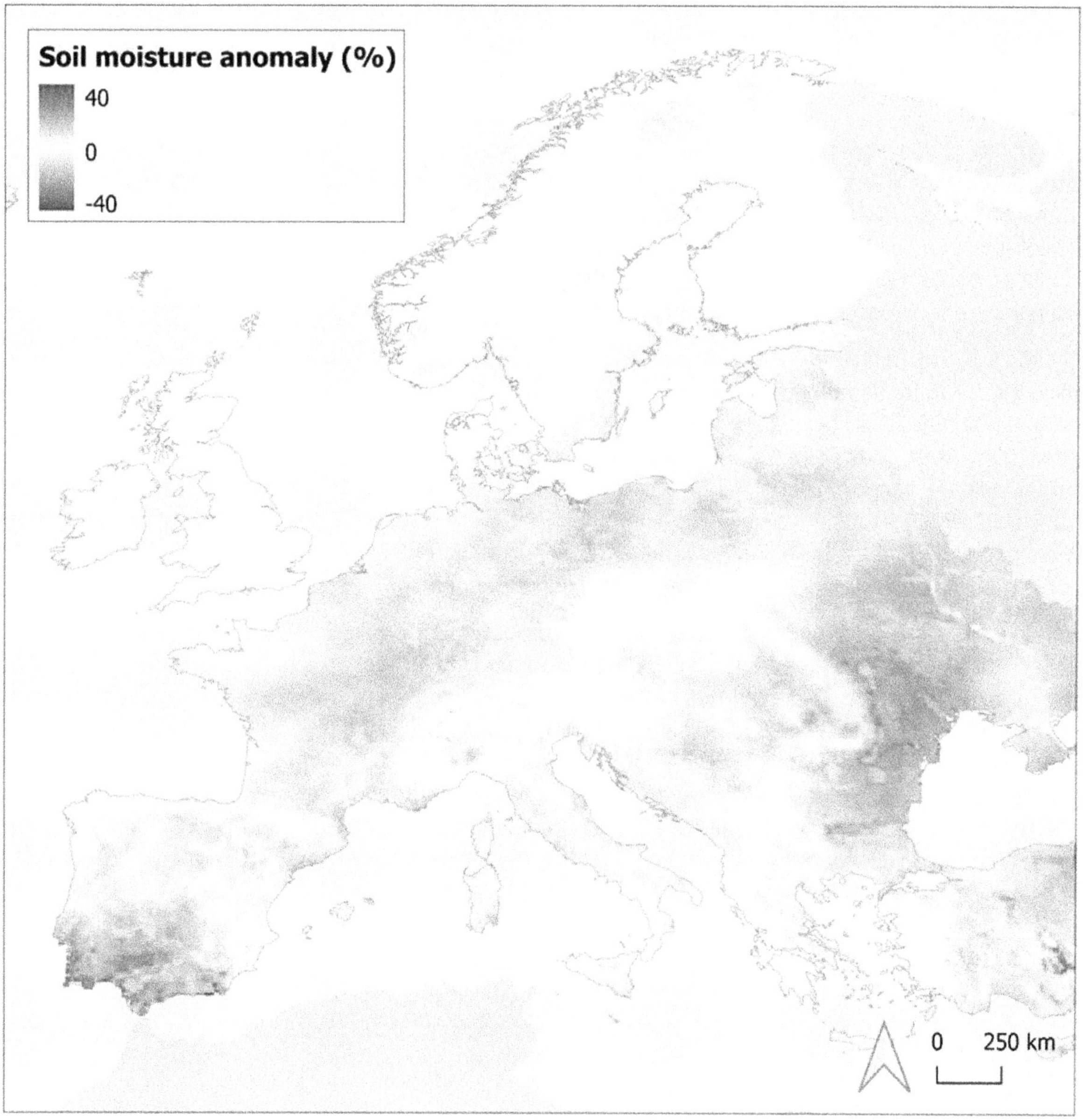

Note: <Negative values indicate increasing drought conditions in the topsoil layer, while positive values indicate wetter conditions in the topsoil layer compared to the reference period 1981-2010.
Source: (Maes et al., 2022[6]).

Record wildfires were experienced in 2023

Wildfires have continued to devastate regions around the world in 2024. This is consistent with global trends and OECD data highlighting that 24.5% of globally burned area between 2019 and 2023 was located in OECD and OECD partner countries. In countries such as Argentina, Australia, Brazil, Colombia, India and South Africa, more than 1% of land area burned each year during this period. This represented more than 660 000 km^2 – roughly equivalent to the size of France. Burning land, whether from wildfires, controlled burning or uncontrolled biomass fires, has far-reaching consequences that hinder efforts to combat climate change and undermine initiatives aimed at mitigating global warming.

In the southern hemisphere, the Brazilian Amazon has experienced its worst six months of wildfires in over 20 years due to historic drought, with 13 489 wildfires recorded (Genot, 2024[20]). Similarly, a record number of fires occurred in the state of São Paulo in August, primarily caused by human activities according to the National Secretary of Protection and Civil Defence (Salati, 2024[21]). It reported significant financial losses, an estimated USD 179 million (R$ 1 billion) for rural producers in the region (Salati, 2024[21]).

In the northern hemisphere, Canada experienced a record-breaking number of wildfires in 2023, with more than 150 000 km^2 of land burned by the end of August. Some fires even continued to smoulder over winter and re-ignited as early as February. Larger wildfires were recorded in Alberta, British Columbia and Manitoba as early as May 2024 (Faguy, 2024[22]). The 2024 wildfire season is now set to have the second-highest carbon emissions on record, following last year's destructive season (CAMS, 2024[23]). Many more wildfires were recorded in Chile, Colombia, Greece, New Zealand, Portugal, Türkiye and the United States.

Wildfires are becoming more widespread, increasing ecosystem damage, notably biodiversity and carbon sinks, and harm to human life. Between 2018 and 2022, about 3.2% of the population in IPAC countries, covering both OECD and OECD partner countries lived in areas with very high or extreme wildfire danger, representing over 160 million people. Countries with the highest population exposure to very high and extreme wildfire danger include South Africa (41.2%), Australia (19%), Costa Rica (12.4%), Brazil (9%) and Chile (8.7%), exposing a combined population of more than 51 million people. In absolute terms, India's population faces the highest overall exposure to wildfires during this period: more than 38 million people live in areas with very high and extreme wildfire danger.

Overall, forests in OECD and partner countries have been more exposed to very high or extreme wildfire danger. For example, in the last five years, Brazil has faced the largest area of forest exposed (~1.9 million km^2) to wildfire danger. Other countries, such as the United States, Australia and Mexico, also have elevated levels of wildfire, with 516 000 km^2, 622 000 km^2 and 614 000 km^2, respectively, exposed to very high or extreme fire risk. Within OECD countries, Israel, Mexico and Portugal have some of the highest percentages, with more than 74% of forest exposed to wildfire danger between 2018 and 2022 (OECD, 2023[24]). These large areas of exposure highlight the considerable risk to forests. Consequently, they should be a policy priority given both human risk and the key role forests play as carbon sinks globally.

Figure 2.8. Increasing forest exposure to wildfire danger

Percentage of forested areas exposed to very high and extreme fire danger for more than three consecutive days, OECD and OECD partner countries, 2000 - 2022

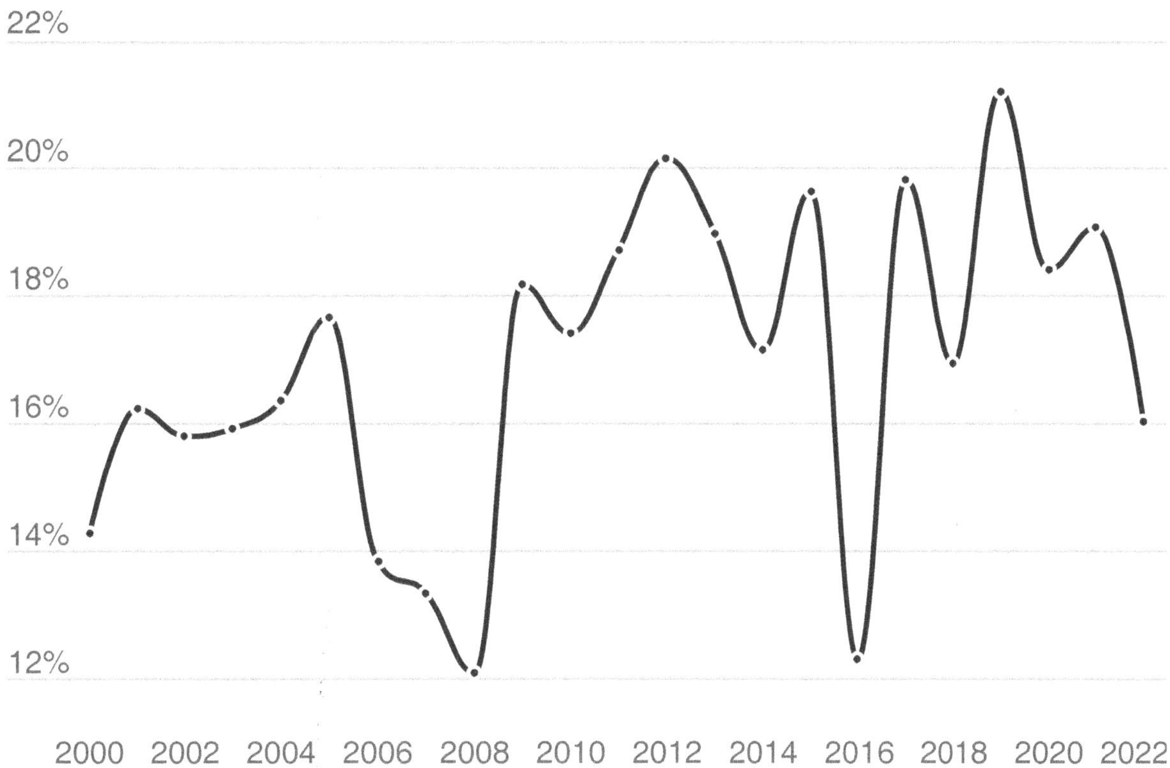

Source: OECD (2024), "Climate-related hazards: Exposure to wildfire", *OECD Environment Statistics* (database), https://oe.cd/dx/58u

Extreme rainfall events continue to cause havoc, resulting in devastating floods and landslides

Heavy rainfall poses significant dangers to countries by causing flash floods, triggering landslides, and potentially affecting both people and economic infrastructure. OECD and partner countries are increasingly exposed to extreme precipitation events for longer periods, with OECD partner countries having a much higher share of land exposed compared to OECD countries (Figure 2.9).

Although most countries monitored by IPAC are exposed to some level of extreme precipitation events, the duration of exposure varies considerably between countries. The OECD and partner countries with the highest share of land exposed to extreme precipitation events between 2019 and 2023 included Indonesia (37.3%), Colombia (28.2%), Peru (22.4%) and Brazil (15.8%).[8] These countries experience higher precipitation due to their location in the tropical region with its warmer temperatures and abundant moisture, among other factors.

Figure 2.9. Exposure to extreme precipitation events in OECD partner countries increased more strongly than in OECD countries

Percentage of land exposed to more than 1 week of extreme precipitation events, OECD and OECD partner countries, 1979-2023.

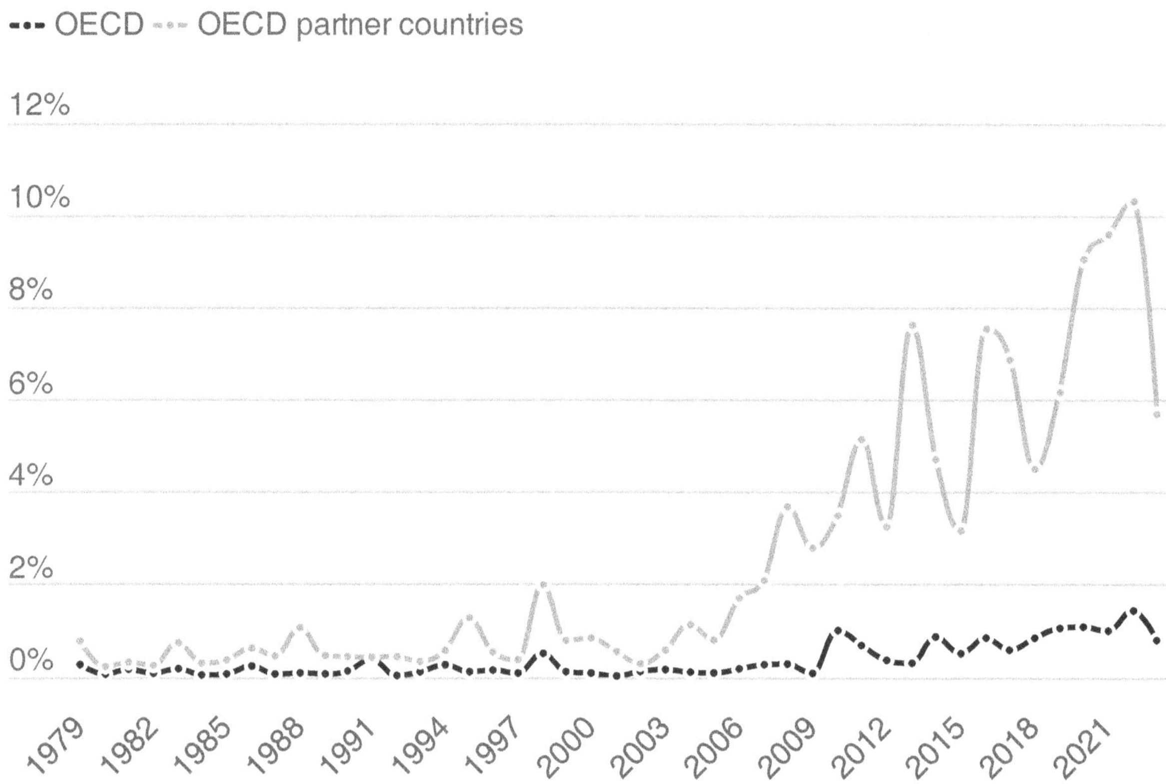

Note: Over- or under-estimations of the estimated exposure to extreme precipitation are possible due to the spatial resolution of gridded data, particularly for smaller countries or regions. A variety of indicators has been developed that estimate exposure to extreme precipitation; these should be consulted for more detailed analysis of individual countries.
Source: IEA/OECD (2024), "Climate-related hazards: Exposure to extreme precipitation", *OECD Environment Statistics* (database), https://oe.cd/dx/58s

Between April and May 2024, large regions in central Asia experienced heavy rainfalls and subsequent flash flooding (Zachariah et al., 2024[25]). This extreme rainfall event was highly unusual, occurring in a so-called hyper-arid region. It was likely worsened due to a combination of human-induced climate change and the El Niño Southern Oscillation in 2023-24 (Zachariah et al., 2024[26]). However, it is difficult to attribute human-induced climate change to specific hazard and disaster events such as this one.

In India, an extreme monsoon rainfall killed hundreds of people due to massive landslides, with the mountainous western Ghats district the worst affected (Zachariah et al., 2024[27]). Across northern Kerala, bridges were washed away, homes and roads were flooded, and power outages occurred. With over 140 mm of rain falling in a single day on already saturated soils, deadly landslides followed (Zachariah et al., 2024[27]). While extreme rainfall events often have localised or regional impacts, they may also have broader national consequences due to the loss of life and economic damage.

In Europe, land exposure to extreme precipitation events remains low (< 2%). However, the wetter-than-average spring of 2024 offered the opportunity to replenish groundwater levels and replenish aquifers over much of western Europe. Record seasonal precipitation was recorded in parts of France, Italy, the Netherlands, Belgium and Ireland (C3S, 2024[28]).

Although dependent on crop types, extreme precipitation events can pose dangers to agriculture by causing flooding, eroding and/or saturating soils, damaging crops, and threatening food production and livelihoods. This can be especially problematic for countries dependent on agriculture. It can make them overly vulnerable to precipitation changes due to climate change.

On average, Indonesia (32.7%), Colombia (12.3%), Peru (10%), Costa Rica (9.8%) and Brazil (3.3%) had the highest share of cropland exposed to extreme precipitation events over 2019-23. The share of cropland exposed to extreme precipitation events has increased for several countries. In Indonesia, for example, such events increased from about 3.4% to 25.2% between 2000-23.

Six of ten countries whose cropland area is most exposed to extreme precipitation events also depend more on agriculture as a share of GDP. For example, Indonesia and Colombia have, on average, about 33% and 12% of cropland, respectively, exposed to extreme precipitation events. Meanwhile, their GDP share of the agriculture, forestry and fishing sector is 12.7% and 6.4%, respectively, which is significantly higher than the average in OECD and OECD partner countries (3.2%).

Flooding is caused by a combination of factors, including extreme precipitation, storm surges, river overflow and more artificial surfaces, and threatens people's lives, livelihoods and economic infrastructure. Among the 51 OECD and OECD partners covered by IPAC, the Netherlands and Hungary have the highest percentage (~20%) of total land area exposed to extreme river flooding. Meanwhile, China is the most exposed country with 22% of its built-up area exposed. China is followed by Latvia (20%) and the Netherlands (18%). In terms of agricultural land, the most affected are Hungary, the Netherlands, and the Slovak Republic with more than 17% of their cropland exposed to possible extreme events.[9]

River flooding can also cause human losses. However, because extreme rainfall and subsequent flooding often have highly localised impacts on populations and infrastructure, many national and subnational indicators may fail to detect these events. In 2023, Europe experienced severe flooding, affecting 1.6 million people across the continent. For example, floods in Italy displaced an estimated 36 000 people and led to 15 fatalities in May. Meanwhile, two-thirds of Slovenia was inundated in August 2023, resulting in six fatalities. Furthermore, record rainfall in Greece, Bulgaria and Türkiye in September 2023, led to 29 deaths and extensive damage, including 700 km^2 of flooded land in Greece (C3S and WMO, 2023[29]). Among the countries monitored, populations in Latvia, the Slovak Republic and the Netherlands are the most exposed, with more than 30% of people potentially affected. Due to the sheer size of China (26%) and India (20%), the total number of people exposed in these two countries to river flooding is about 670 million (Figure 2.10).

Figure 2.10. Population exposure to river flooding varies between OECD and OECD partner countries

Percentage of population exposed to river flooding, with a return period of 100 years, OECD and OECD partner countries, 2020

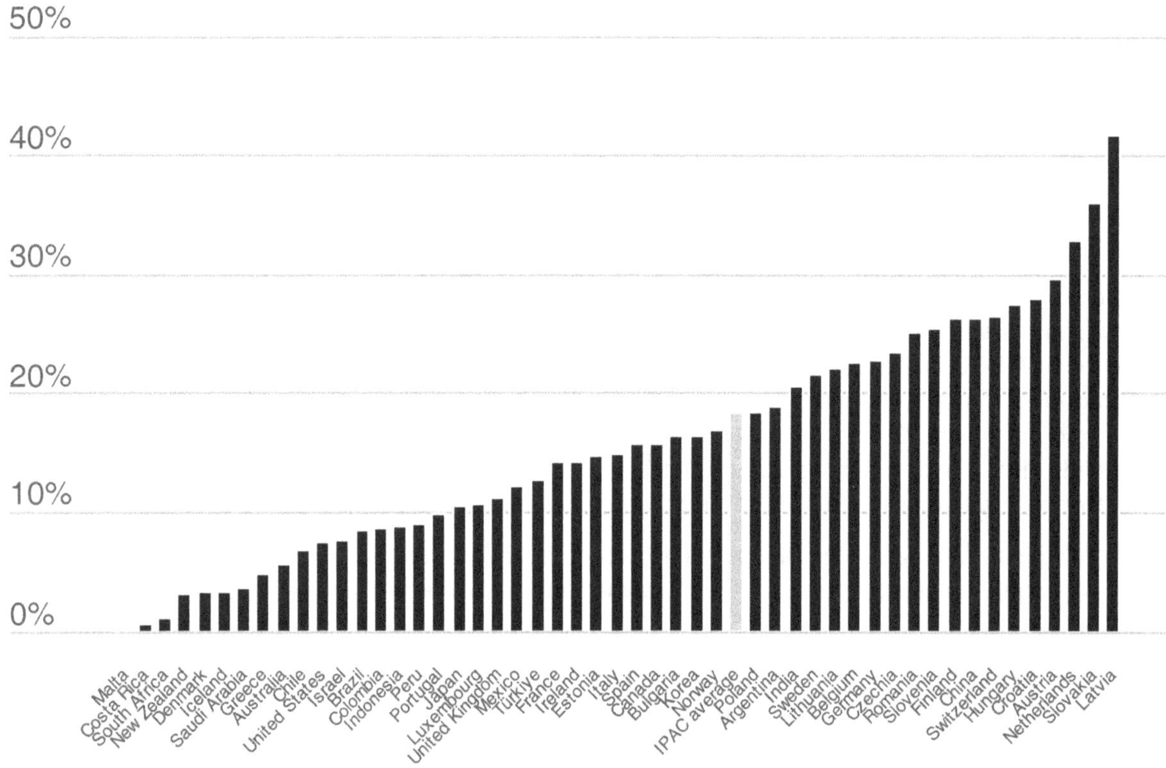

Source: OECD (2024), "Climate-related hazards: Exposure to river flooding", *OECD Environment Statistics* (database), https://oe.cd/dx/58w

Low-lying coastal communities face a range of coastal flooding hazards such as storm surges and erosion. These hazards are expected to worsen as climate change increases the frequency and severity of coastal floods. The most exposed countries are the Netherlands, Belgium and Denmark. In the Netherlands, 51% of land area is potentially exposed to coastal flooding with a ten-year return period, followed by 6.4% for Belgium and 5.6% for Denmark. However, these figures should be interpreted with caution as they do not consider existing flood protection measures or sea-level rise. Nevertheless, they underscore the importance of maintaining protections to prevent future impacts and the potential economic costs of damage caused by climate change.

Built-up area exposure to coastal flooding is increasing. Across the countries covered by IPAC, the percentage of built-up area exposed to coastal flooding increased from 1.8% in 2000 to 2.6% in 2020.This suggests that additional investment in infrastructure will be necessary, particularly if built-up areas continue to expand in coastal zones. The most affected is the Netherlands that has 52% of its built-up area exposed to coastal flooding, followed by Belgium (10%) and China (6.6%). Much of the land along the North Sea coast is either below sea level or just slightly above it. This exposes a sizeable amount of the land and its built-up areas to coastal flooding hazards.

Figure 2.11. Built-up area expansion in coastal zones increases coastal flooding exposure

Percentage of built-up area exposed to coastal flooding with a 100-year return period, OECD and OECD Partner countries average, 2000-2022.

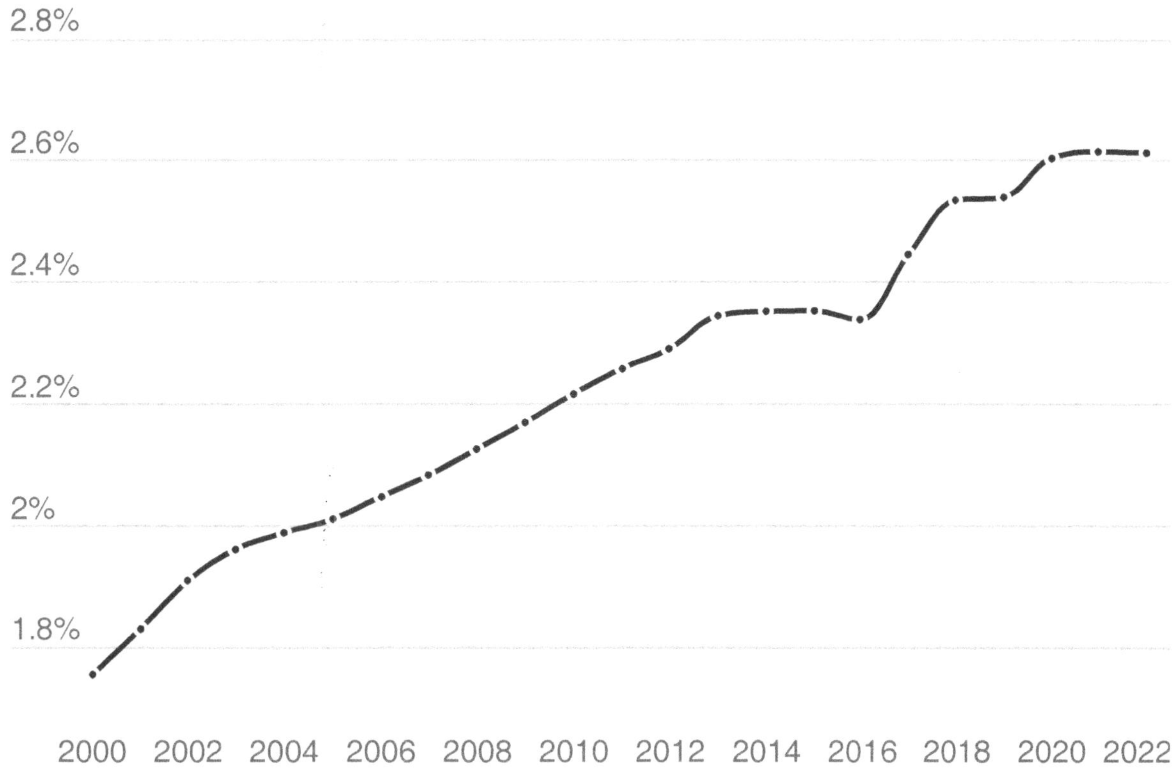

Source: OECD (2024), "Climate-related hazards: Exposure to coastal flooding", *OECD Environment Statistics* (database), https://oe.cd/dx/58x

The hurricane season of 2024 will likely break records due to climate change and La Niña

Storms and cyclones affect all countries covered by IPAC with varying degrees of intensity and occurrence, and at times worsen the effects of other hazards. According to the National Oceanic and Atmospheric Administration, the 2024 hurricane season (1 June to 30 November) will be exceptionally active due to a combination of warmer ocean temperature and a La Niña climate pattern (Jones, 2024[30]). Hurricane Beryl became the earliest forming a Category 5 Atlantic hurricane in recorded history, and the second such storm in July (WMO, 2024[31]). This highlights how warmer ocean temperatures due to climate change risks facilitating cyclogenesis (Knutson et al., 2021[32]).

Countries most exposed to violent storms are located principally in northwest Europe and East Asia. In countries such as Belgium, Iceland, Ireland and the Netherlands, more than 40% of the population and built-up areas were exposed to violent storms in 2019-23 (Figure 2.12). Meanwhile, exposure to tropical cyclones is limited to a subset of countries covered by IPAC due to their geographic position. The most exposed of these countries are Japan and Korea (90%) where more than 90% of their populations and built-up areas are exposed to tropical cyclones (with wind speeds higher than 119 km/h or 33 m/s). These two countries are followed by Mexico and China with 25%.

Figure 2.12. Populations in northwestern Europe and East Asia are particularly exposed to violent windstorms

Percentage of population exposed to violent windstorms, OECD and OECD partner countries, 2019-23 average

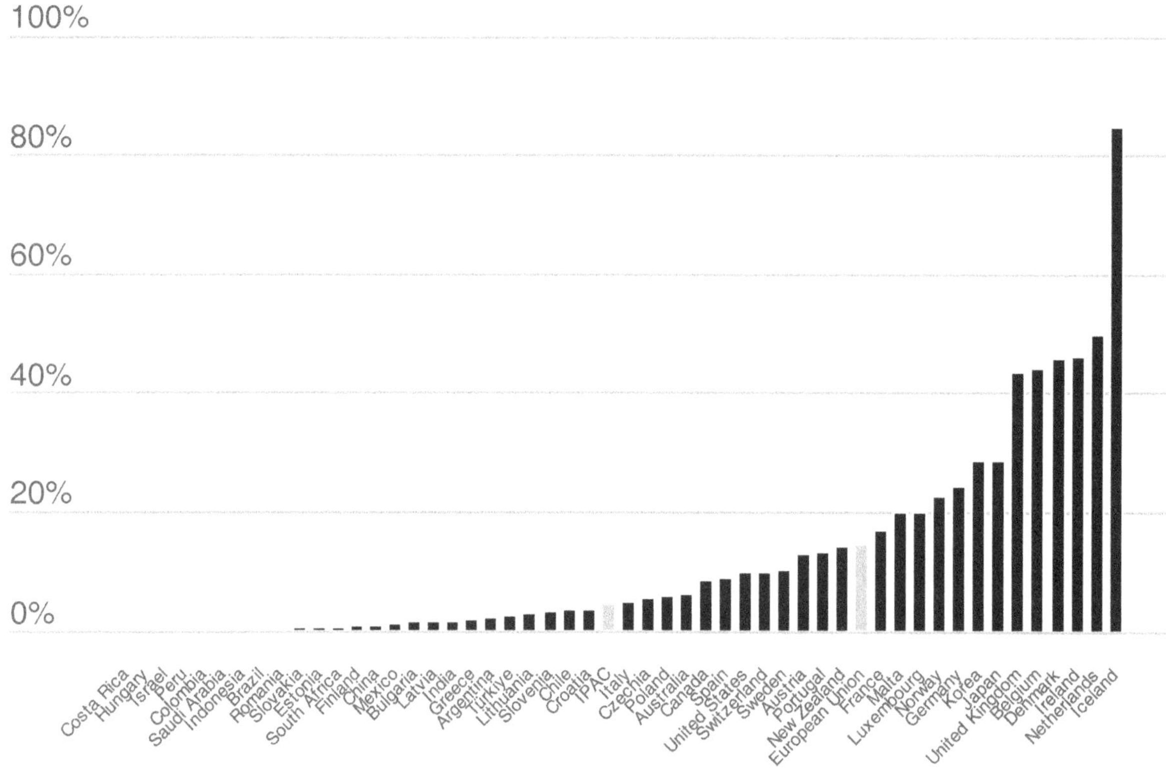

Source: OECD (2024), "Climate-related hazards: Exposure to wind threats", *OECD Environment Statistics* (database), https://oe.cd/dx/58v

Economic losses and deaths due to climate disasters

Extreme weather events exacerbate social, political and economic stressors, such as food insecurity. The trajectory of future changes in climate remains uncertain. However, increasing severity of extreme weather events, along with increasing population density in hazard-prone locations, is likely to lead to rising climate-related catastrophic losses (OECD, 2021[33]).

Annual economic losses due to climate-related disasters change from year to year. However, economic losses have tended to increase across IPAC countries since the 1990s (Figure 2.13). Similarly, economic losses due to weather, climate and water extremes have reportedly increased sevenfold from the 1970s to the 2010s (WMO, 2021[34]). Storms are responsible for the largest economic damages (more than USD 2.3 trillion between 1990 and 2023), followed by damages from floods, droughts, wildfires and extreme temperatures (Figure 2.13). Hurricane Harvey in 2017 and Hurricane Ian in 2022 caused estimated economic losses of more than USD 118 billion and USD 104 billion, respectively, in the United States, making them some of the costliest storms on record.

Figure 2.13. Economic losses due to climate disasters increase, with largest losses due to storms, floods and droughts

Total economic losses, thousand USD (adjusted), OECD and OECD partner countries, 1990-2023

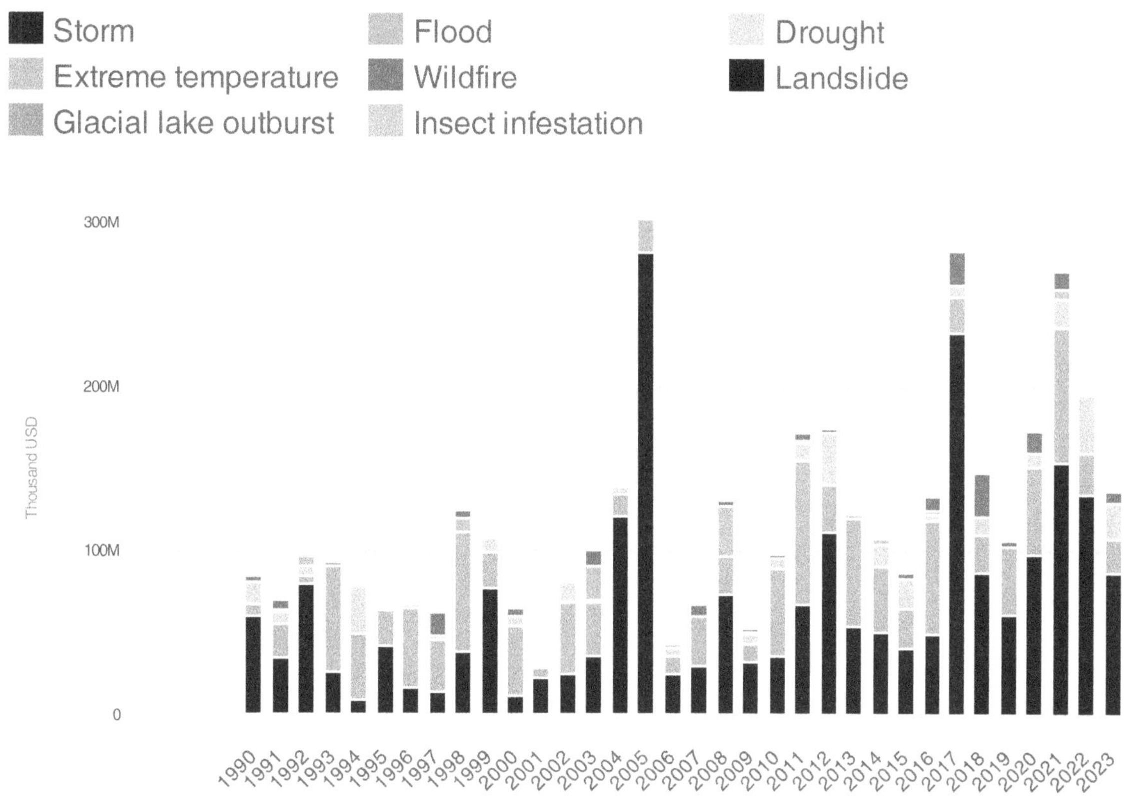

Note: Many disaster databases suffer from limited spatial coverage, which leads to under-estimations of the loss of life and damages incurred due to climate-related disasters and potentially results in reporting gaps for certain countries.
Source: OECD calculations based on data from EM-DAT, CRED / UCLouvain, Brussels, Belgium, – www.emdat.be

Loss of life due to climate-related disasters is spread differently than economic losses. Extreme temperatures cause a vast majority of deaths related to climate-related disasters. In 2022, for example, a heatwave event in Italy and Spain caused more than 29 000 deaths (Figure 2.14). This illustrates that climate-related disasters with high economic losses are not necessarily the same ones with the highest loss of life.

Figure 2.14. The largest losses of life are due to heatwave events, followed by floods and storms

Total deaths, OECD and OECD partner countries, 1990-2023

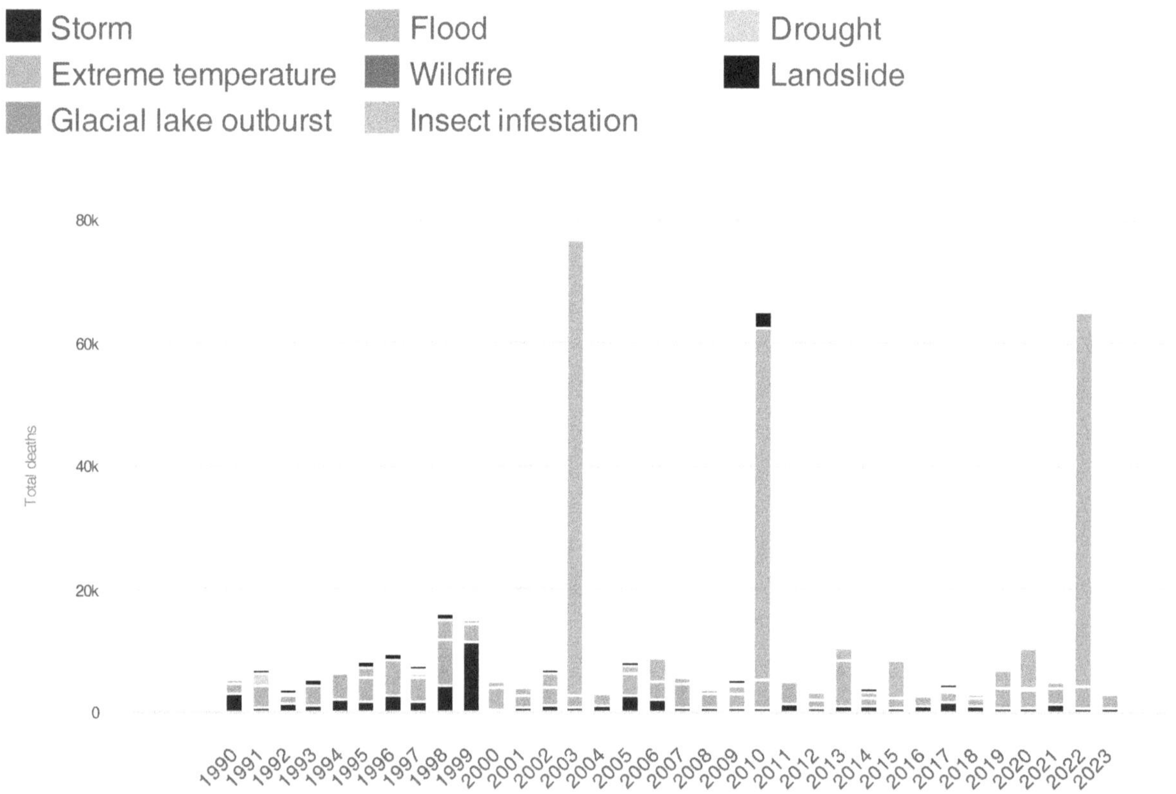

Note: Many disaster databases suffer from limited spatial coverage, which leads to under-estimations of the loss of life and damages incurred due to climate-related disasters and potentially results in reporting gaps for certain countries.
Source: OECD calculations based on data from EM-DAT, CRED / UCLouvain, Brussels, Belgium, www.emdat.be

Developing countries, including Least Developed Countries and Small Island Developing States, are disproportionately affected by the impacts of extreme weather events. This is due to their lower levels of development and economic diversification, fiscal constraints and physical characteristics, among other reasons (OECD, 2021[33]). Due to limited spatial coverage of disasters databases and the under reporting of damages and lives lost, many of these countries have a significant reporting gap (Moriyama, Sasaki and Ono, 2018[35]). The African continent, for example, saw 35% of deaths related to weather, climate and water extremes but just 1% of reported global economic losses (WMO, 2021[36]). These disparities highlight the urgent need for improved data collection and reporting mechanisms to accurately assess the impact of extreme weather events in developing countries and to inform effective climate adaptation strategies.

Evidence in many countries monitored by IPAC confirms that accelerated action on adaptation is needed to contain future loss and damage. Investments in climate adaptation measures are usually significantly less expensive than addressing loss and damage from extreme weather events. For example, one study shows that investing USD 1.8 trillion globally in five areas from 2020 to 2030 could generate USD 7.1 trillion in total net benefits (GCA, 2019[37]). However, government funding is usually only made available after a disaster. This gives rise to important considerations for adaptation finance (OECD, 2023[38]).

Box 2.2. Fund for responding to loss and damage

The 28th session of the Conference of the Parties (COP28), held in Dubai in November and December 2023, led to the formal establishment and operationalisation of the Fund for responding to Loss and Damage. This Fund is set to provide assistance to those countries most vulnerable to, and affected by, the effects of climate change.

Several countries have pledged money to the Fund, including the United Arab Emirates, France, Germany, the United Kingdom and the United States, among others. At its first Board Meeting in April 2024, the Board decided the Philippines would be the host country of the Fund.

To kick start the new funding arrangements, a transitional committee was convened to prepare recommendations for adoption at COP28 in November 2023. It considered the following elements:

- establishing institutional arrangements, modalities, structure, governance and terms of reference for the Fund
- defining the elements of the new funding arrangements
- identifying and expanding sources of funding
- ensuring co-ordination and complementarity with existing funding arrangements.

The Loss and Damage Fund should fill gaps left by current climate finance institutions such as the Green Climate Fund and Adaptation Fund. Campaigners argue that the Loss and Damage Fund must be accountable to the most vulnerable, drawing on the experience of community-based organisations, and favouring grants rather than loans. Financing instruments that could be used to provide a buffer and rapid pay-outs after disasters include social protection, contingency finance, catastrophe risk insurance and catastrophe bonds. However, a broadened donor base and innovative finance tools would be needed to respond to the magnitude of loss and damage.

Source: (UNFCCC, 2023[39]).

Strong climate mitigation efforts are needed to avoid triggering climate tipping points that risk fundamentally changing regional and global climate

The pace of climate change increases the intensity and occurrence of extreme weather events. Climate change risks also further accelerating climate tipping points that disrupt stable climate patterns and amplify climate disturbances on a continental and global scale. Climate tipping points are reached when a change in part of the climate system goes beyond a certain threshold that results in an abrupt and potentially irreversible impact (OECD, 2022[40]).

The risks of climate tipping points, the disintegration of the Greenland Ice sheet, the melting of the Arctic Permafrost or the weakening of ocean circulations cannot be overstated. Evidence shows that under current pledges the world is heading towards 2-3°C of global warming and will likely trigger multiple climate tipping points (Figure 2.15). Climate tipping points interact with each other and can influence the likelihood of triggering another tipping point, creating an unstoppable climate tipping cascade. Allowing for a climate tipping cascade to occur puts the planet in a "state of planetary emergency" (Lenton et al., 2019[41]). Limiting global warming to 1.5°C is crucial to avoid the possibility of accelerating more catastrophic impacts of combined climate tipping points (OECD, 2022[40]).

Figure 2.15. Current global warming may already trigger certain climate tipping points, and become increasingly likely with further warming

Location of climate tipping elements in the cryosphere (blue), biosphere (green) and ocean/atmosphere (orange), and global warming levels at which these tipping points will likely be triggered.

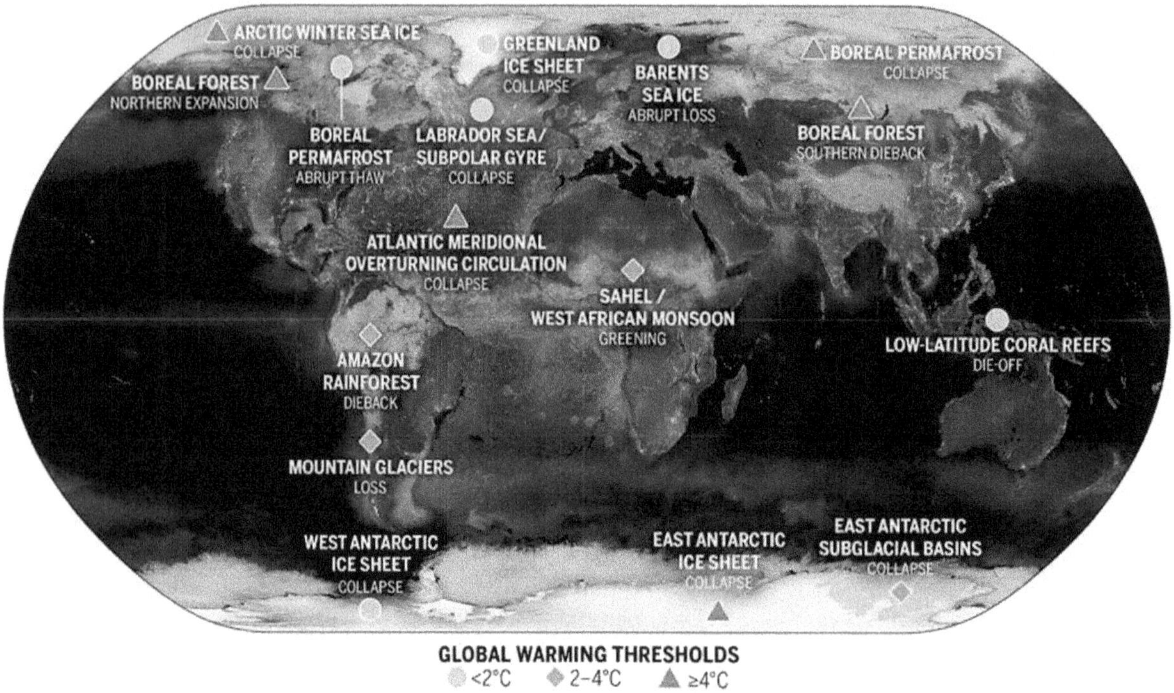

Source: Illustration from (Armstrong McKay et al., 2022[42]).

References

Armstrong McKay, D. et al. (2022), "Exceeding 1.5 C global warming could trigger multiple climate tipping points", *Science*, Vol. 377/6611, https://doi.org/10.1126/science.abn7950. [42]

C3S (2024), "New record daily global average temperature reached in July 2024", 25 July, Copernicus Climate Change Service, https://climate.copernicus.eu/new-record-daily-global-average-temperature-reached-july-2024#:~:text=Last%2022%20July%202024%20was,virtual%20tie%20at%2017.15%C2%BAC. [12]

C3S (2024), "Precipitation, relative humidity and soil moisture for May 2024", Copernicus Climate Change Service, https://climate.copernicus.eu/precipitation-relative-humidity-and-soil-moisture-may-2024#:~:text=May%202024%20was%20wetter%20than,and%20Italy%2C%20amongst%20other%20regions. (accessed on 23 August 2024). [28]

C3S and WMO (2023), *European State of the Climate 2023*, (database), https://climate.copernicus.eu/esotc/2023 (accessed on 23 August 2024). [29]

CAMS (2024), "Summer wildfires and record emissions in the Americas", 2 August, Copernicus Atmosphere Monitoring Service, https://atmosphere.copernicus.eu/summer-wildfires-and-record-emissions-americas. [23]

Climate Change Knowledge Portal (2024), *CCKP*, website, https://climateknowledgeportal.worldbank.org/ (accessed on 14 June 2024). [17]

CRED (2024), *2023 Disasters in Numbers*, Centre for Research on the Epidemiology of Disasters, University of Louvain, Brussels, https://files.emdat.be/reports/2023_EMDAT_report.pdf. [5]

CSE (2024), "Urban heat stress tracke – Delhi", 23 May, Centre for Science and Environment, New Delhi, https://www.cseindia.org/urban-heat-stress-tracker-delhi-12193. [15]

Euronews Green (2024), "Mexico is so hot that monkeys, birds and bats are falling dead from trees", https://www.euronews.com/green/2024/05/28/mexico-is-so-hot-that-monkeys-birds-and-bats-are-falling-dead-from-trees (accessed on 20 August 2024). [43]

Faguy, A. (2024), "Thousands told to evacuate due to British Columbia, Canada wildfire", BBC News, 11 May, https://www.bbc.com/news/world-us-canada-68996062. [22]

GCA (2019), *Adapt Now: A Global Call for Leadership on Climate Resilience*, Global Center on Adaptation, Rotterdam, https://gca.org/reports/adapt-now-a-global-call-for-leadership-on-climate-resilience/. [37]

Genot, L. (2024), "Brazil's Amazon sees worst 6 months of wildfires in 20 years", 2 July, phys.org, https://phys.org/news/2024-07-brazil-amazon-worst-months-wildfires.html. [20]

Gidden, M. et al. (2019), "Global emissions pathways under different socioeconomic scenarios for use in CMIP6: A dataset of harmonized emissions trajectories through the end of the century", *Geoscientific Model Development*, Vol. 12/4, pp. 1443-1475, https://doi.org/10.5194/gmd-12-1443-2019. [11]

IPCC (2022), *Climate Change 2022: Impacts, Adaptation and Vulnerability*, Intergovernmental Panel on Climate Change, Geneva, https://report.ipcc.ch/ar6wg2/pdf/IPCC_AR6_WGII_FinalDraft_FullReport.pdf. [1]

IPCC (2021), *Climate Change 2021: The Physical Science Basis. Contribution of Working Group I to the Sixth Assessment Report of the Intergovernmental Panel on Climate Change*, Intergovernmental Panel on Climate Change, Geneva. [13]

Jones, J. (2024), "The 2024 hurricane season could be a dangerous one", 24 May, https://www.scientificamerican.com/article/the-2024-hurricane-season-could-be-a-dangerous-one/#:~:text=The%20record%202020%20hurricane%20season,expect%20to%20see%20in%202024.&text=It%20is%20also%20important%20to,warm%20ocean%20to%20fuel%20them. [30]

Knutson, T. et al. (2021), "Climate change is probably increasing the intensity of tropical cyclones", *Zenodo*, https://zenodo.org/records/4570334. [32]

Lenton, T. et al. (2019), "Climate tipping points — too risky to bet against", *Nature*, Vol. 575/7784, pp. 592-595. [41]

Maes, M. et al. (2022), “Monitoring exposure to climate-related hazards: Indicator methodology and key results”, *OECD Environment Working Papers*, No. 201, OECD Publishing, Paris, https://doi.org/10.1787/da074cb6-en. [6]

Moriyama, K., D. Sasaki and Y. Ono (2018), “Comparison of global databases for disaster loss and damage data”, *Journal of Disaster Research*, Vol. 13/6, pp. 1007-1014, https://doi.org/10.20965/jdr.2018.p1007. [35]

Munich RE (2024), “Record Thunderstorm Losses and Deadly Earthquakes: The Natural Disasters of 2023”, webpage, https://www.munichre.com/en/company/media-relations/media-information-and-corporate-news/media-information/2024/natural-disaster-figures-2023.html (accessed on 8 July 2024). [2]

Munich RE (2023), “Climate Change and La Niña Driving Losses: The Natural Disaster Figures for 2022”, webpage, https://www.munichre.com/en/company/media-relations/media-information-and-corporate-news/media-information/2023/natural-disaster-figures-2022.html#:~:text=2022%20natural%20disasters%20in%20figures,of%20years%20with%20high%20losses. (accessed on 20 July 2023). [3]

Munich RE (2022), “Hurricanes, Cold Waves, Tornadoes: Weather Disasters in USA Dominate Natural Disaster Losses in 2021”, webpage, https://www.munichre.com/en/company/media-relations/media-information-and-corporate-news/media-information/2022/natural-disaster-losses-2021.html (accessed on 10 June 2022). [4]

OECD (2023), *OECD Environmental Performance Reviews: Germany 2023*, OECD Environmental Performance Reviews, OECD Publishing, Paris, https://doi.org/10.1787/f26da7da-en. [38]

OECD (2023), *OECD Environmental Performance Reviews: Portugal 2023*, OECD Environmental Performance Reviews, OECD Publishing, Paris, https://doi.org/10.1787/d9783cbf-en. [24]

OECD (2022), *Climate Tipping Points: Insights for Effective Policy Action*, OECD Publishing, Paris, https://doi.org/10.1787/abc5a69e-en. [40]

OECD (2021), *Managing Climate Risks, Facing up to Losses and Damages*, OECD Publishing, Paris, https://doi.org/10.1787/55ea1cc9-en. [33]

Page, M. (2024), “Deaths during annual Hajj in Saudi Arabia underscore extreme heat dangers”, 6 June, Human Rights Watch, https://www.hrw.org/news/2024/06/25/deaths-during-annual-hajj-saudi-arabia-underscore-extreme-heat-dangers. [16]

Riahi, K. et al. (2017), “The Shared Socioeconomic Pathways and their energy, land use, and greenhouse gas emissions implications: An overview”, *Global Environmental Change*, Vol. 42, pp. 153-168, https://doi.org/10.1016/J.GLOENVCHA.2016.05.009. [9]

Rogelj, J. et al. (2018), “Scenarios towards limiting global mean temperature increase below 1.5 C”, *Nature Climate Change*, Vol. 8/4, pp. 325-332, https://doi.org/10.1038/s41558-018-0091-3. [10]

Salati, P. (2024), "Onda de incêndios em SP provocou perdas de R$ 1 bilhão na agropecuária, diz governo estadual", [Wave of fires in SP caused losses of R$1 billion in agriculture, says state government], g1, https://g1.globo.com/economia/agronegocios/noticia/2024/08/26/onda-de-incendios-em-sp-provocou-perdas-de-r-1-bilhao-na-agropecuaria-diz-governo-estadual.ghtml (accessed on 29 August 2024). [21]

Seltenrich, N. (2023), "No reprieve: Extreme heat at night contributes to heat wave mortality", *Environmental Health Perspectives*, Vol. 131/7, https://doi.org/10.1289/EHP13206. [18]

Swiss Re (2021), *The Economics of Climate Change: No Action not an Option*, Swiss Re Institute, Zurich, https://www.swissre.com/dam/jcr:e73ee7c3-7f83-4c17-a2b8-8ef23a8d3312/swiss-re-institute-expertise-publication-economics-of-climate-change.pdf. [7]

Tebaldi, C. and R. Knutti (2007), "The use of the multi-model ensemble in probabilistic climate projections", *Philosophical Transactions of the Royal Society A: Mathematical, Physical and Engineering Sciences*, Vol. 365/1857, pp. 2053-2075, https://doi.org/10.1098/RSTA.2007.2076. [8]

The Guardian (2024), "Unprecedented number of heat records broken around world this year", 14 August, The Guardian, https://www.theguardian.com/environment/article/2024/aug/14/unprecedented-number-of-heat-records-broken-around-world-this-year (accessed on 20 August 2024). [14]

UNFCCC (2023), *Transitional Committee*, webpage, https://unfccc.int/topics/adaptation-and-resilience/groups-committees/transitional-committee. [39]

WMO (2024), "Record-breaking Hurricane Beryl threatens Caribbean", 8 July, World Meteorological Organization, Geneva, https://wmo.int/media/news/record-breaking-hurricane-beryl-threatens-caribbean (accessed on 28 August 2024). [31]

WMO (2021), *Atlas of Mortality and Economic Losses from Weather, Climate and Water Extremes (1970-2019)*, World Meteorological Organization, Geneva. [34]

WMO (2021), *State of the Global Climate 2020*, World Meteorological Organization, Geneva. [36]

World Bank (2018), *Romania: Systematic Country Diagnostic*, World Bank, Washington, DC. [19]

Zachariah, M. et al. (2024), "Landslide-triggering rainfall made more intense by human-induced climate change, devastating highly vulnerable communities in northern Kerala", Imperial College London, https://doi.org/10.25561/113860. [27]

Zachariah, M. et al. (2024), "Heavy precipitation hitting vulnerable communities in the UAE and Oman becoming an increasing threat as the climate warms", Imperial College London, https://spiral.imperial.ac.uk/handle/10044/1/110910. [26]

Zachariah, M. et al. (2024), "Increasing April-May rainfall, El Niño and high vulnerability behind deadly flooding in Afghanistan, Pakistan and Iran", Imperial College London, https://doi.org/10.25561/112169. [25]

Notes

[1] Including non-climate related disasters such as earthquakes.

[2] Absolute thresholds used to determine hot days can vary from 30 °C to 50 °C, depending on their use. More complex indicators, such as the Universal Thermal Climate Index, can describe extreme heat, combining other factors such as moisture, wind and solar radiation to account for a more thorough analysis to heat exposure for individual countries.

[3] Hot days are defined as those during which daily maximum temperature surpasses 35 °C. Due to the resolution of the raw data, extreme heat for small islands may be slightly under-estimated. There are also several additional indicators to describe extreme heat (such as the Universal Thermal Climate Index, which also considers moisture, wind and solar radiation); these should be considered for a more thorough analysis of exposure to heat for single countries.

[4] For example, in June 2024, more than 1 300 Muslims died during the annual pilgrimage to Mecca, as temperatures soared above 50 °C. Reportedly, 83% of these fatalities involved unregistered pilgrims, who sought to avoid high pilgrimage costs. In the case of wildlife a strong high pressure system in May 2024 over the southern Gulf of Mexico caused a heat dome, where howler monkeys and other wildlife died due to dehydration (Euronews Green, 2024[43]).

[5] By using a multi-model perspective consisting of up to 30 climate models, reliable climate projections that capture uncertainty provide insights on future changes of key hazards such as hot days.

[6] Tropical nights are defined as nights where the minimum temperature does not fall below 20 °C. Due to the resolution of the raw data, extreme heat exposure for small islands may be slightly over- or under-estimated. There are also several additional indicators to describe extreme heat (such as the UTCI), which also takes moisture, wind and solar radiation into account); these should be considered for a more thorough analysis of exposure to heat for single countries.

[7] Annual population exposure to more than eight weeks of tropical nights.

[8] Extreme precipitation is defined here as precipitation of more than one week.

[9] River flooding events are defined in terms of a 100-year flooding event.

3 How far did countries' climate action progress?

Effective climate action plays a critical role in complying with countries' national commitments and achieving net-zero targets. In 2023, only a modest expansion of 2% in countries' climate policy effort was recorded. To achieve the Paris Agreement temperature goals, climate action must increase significantly. Chapter 1 of this report showed that current Nationally Determined Contributions (NDCs) and net-zero targets are not in line with limiting global warming to 1.5°C or 2°C, indicating an ambition gap. According to the first Global Stocktake[1], policies implemented by the end of 2020 were insufficient to meet countries' NDCs, indicating an implementation gap as well (UNFCCC, 2023[1]).

This section provides a snapshot of key developments in climate policies in 2023 based on the Climate Actions and Policies Measurement Framework (CAPMF) developed under the International Programme for Action on Climate (IPAC).[2] The CAPMF tracks trends in climate mitigation action of governments by considering both adoption and stringency (i.e. the degree to which policies incentivise or enable GHG emission reduction)[3] of policies for OECD and partner countries, excluding the USA (Nachtigall et al., 2022[2]). It identifies 130 policies covering a broad range of instrument types (e.g. market-based, non-market-based) and other climate policy actions (e.g. climate targets, climate governance, climate data). These account for around 75% of the instruments listed in the Intergovernmental Panel on Climate Change (IPCC) Sixth Assessment Report (IPCC, 2022[3]). Moreover, the CAPMF also covers important sector-specific policies responsible for around 89% of greenhouse (GHG) emissions in OECD and OECD partner countries.

The primary objective of the CAPMF is to track the evolution and stringency of government national climate mitigation policies over time (1990 to 2023). It collects a broad set of harmonised data that is internationally comparable and suitable for a broad-based quantitative and qualitative analysis. However, it has some limitations and, hence, should be interpreted carefully. [4] First, the coverage is not global; it covers 50 jurisdictions including the European Union as a bloc. It considers all countries covered under IPAC except the United States, since the CAPMF does not fully capture its climate action. Second, due to data availability constraints, the CAPMF does not collect data on all policies, for example, it does not fully capture new climate policies such as carbon abatement payment or pledges (e.g. Global Renewables and Energy Efficiency Pledge) (COP28 UAE, 2023[4]) nor does it include ETS II, which will only become fully operational by 2027. Efforts are underway to expand the policy coverage of the CAPMF to better reflect countries' policy approaches and capture more recent policy developments. Finally, the results of the CAPMF should be interpreted in a descriptive rather than prescriptive way (see Annex for more details).

Notwithstanding these limitations, the CAPMF is a valuable database that provides insights into increasingly complex and varied climate policy approaches across countries. It has already been used in several studies and served as a foundation for evidence-based policy recommendations (D'Arcangelo, Kruse and Pisu, 2023[5]; Stechemesser et al., 2024[6]).

The expansion of climate mitigation policy action has slowed

In 2023, national climate mitigation policy action, as measured by the CAPMF, only expanded by 2% across OECD and OECD partner countries (Figure 3.1). While this is more than the 1% observed in the previous year (OECD, 2023[7]), it still falls short of the 10% annual average expansion in climate policy action between 2010 and 2020. Climate policy action is measured as a combination of policy density and policy stringency.[5] In 2023, the increase in climate policy action was driven principally by the strengthening of existing policies; countries adopted few new policies.

Figure 3.1. In 2023, climate policy action only expanded by 2% driven by the strengthening of existing policies

Number of adopted policies by policy stringency, OECD and OECD Partner countries 2010-2023

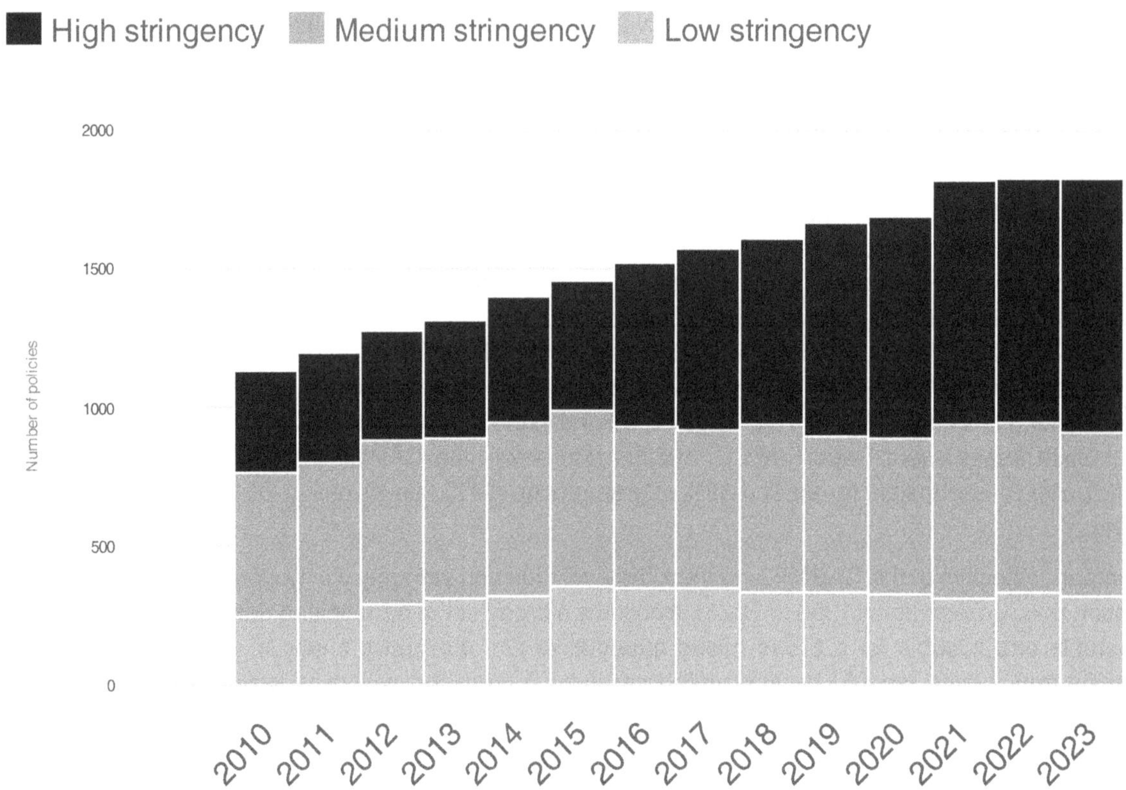

Definition: Policy stringency is the degree to which climate actions and policies incentivise or enable GHG emissions mitigation. It is based on the in-sample distribution of the underlying policy level across all countries and all years.

Note: Low stringency is defined as a score of 0-3, medium as 4-7 and high as 8-10.

Source: Based on data from OECD, IEA, ITF, World Bank and others using the methodology of Nachtigall, D. et al. (2022): "The climate actions and policies measurement framework: A structured and harmonised climate policy database to monitor countries' mitigation action", OECD Environment Working Papers, No. 203, OECD Publishing, Paris, https://doi.org/10.1787/2caa60ce-en

The following sections provide details on the areas where climate policy action expanded and where it did not. The modest expansion in national climate mitigation policy action in 2023 reflects many different, at times opposing, policy developments across country groups, sectors, and instrument types. Generally, climate policy action expanded in most countries but declined in a few. Notably, climate policy action contracted slightly in the electricity sector but rebounded in the transport, buildings and – most strongly – industry sector after a decrease in 2022. Climate policy action grew strongly for non-market-based instruments (nMBIs) such as standards. Meanwhile, market-based instruments (MBIs) such as carbon pricing and subsidies declined slightly, continuing the slowdown of recent years.

This modest expansion of climate policy action underscores the need for governments to intensify efforts to fulfil their NDCs and achieve the Paris Agreement temperature goals. While climate policy action – as measured by the CAPMF – does not directly measure the effectiveness of these policies, recent evidence suggests a positive relationship between the expansion of climate policy action and emissions reductions (Nachtigall et al., 2024[8]). Specifically, the average change of climate action between 2015 and 2020 has been associated with a 13% reduction in emissions (Nachtigall et al., 2024[8]). Extrapolating these results suggests that countries must expand climate action to meet their NDCs and to be on track with the Paris Agreement temperature goals (IPCC, 2022[3]). Countries retain multiple options to accelerate climate action by strengthening existing policies or introducing new initiatives.

The expansion of climate mitigation policy action was mostly driven by increases in policy stringency

In recent years, the expansion of climate mitigation policy action was driven by the strengthening of existing policies rather than due to adoption of new ones. Between 2010 and 2022, more than half of the aggregate expansion of climate policy action can be attributed to the adoption of new policies (Figure 3.2). However, in 2023, policy adoption was responsible for only 10% of the expansion in climate policy action whereas strengthening existing policies accounted for 90%. This finding underscores the critical importance of tracking policy stringency. It would not be possible to recognise a significant expansion in climate action based on increased intensity by only tracking policy adoption, for example, the expansion of climate action in the European Union based on the increasing price of GHG emissions in EU Emissions Trading System (EU ETS) after its implementation in 2005 would be undetected, although prices increased from EUR 5 to EUR 80.

Figure 3.2. In recent years the expansion of climate policy action is driven by the strengthening of existing policies

Growth of climate action associated with policy adoption and policy stringency: 2010 = 100; 2010-2023

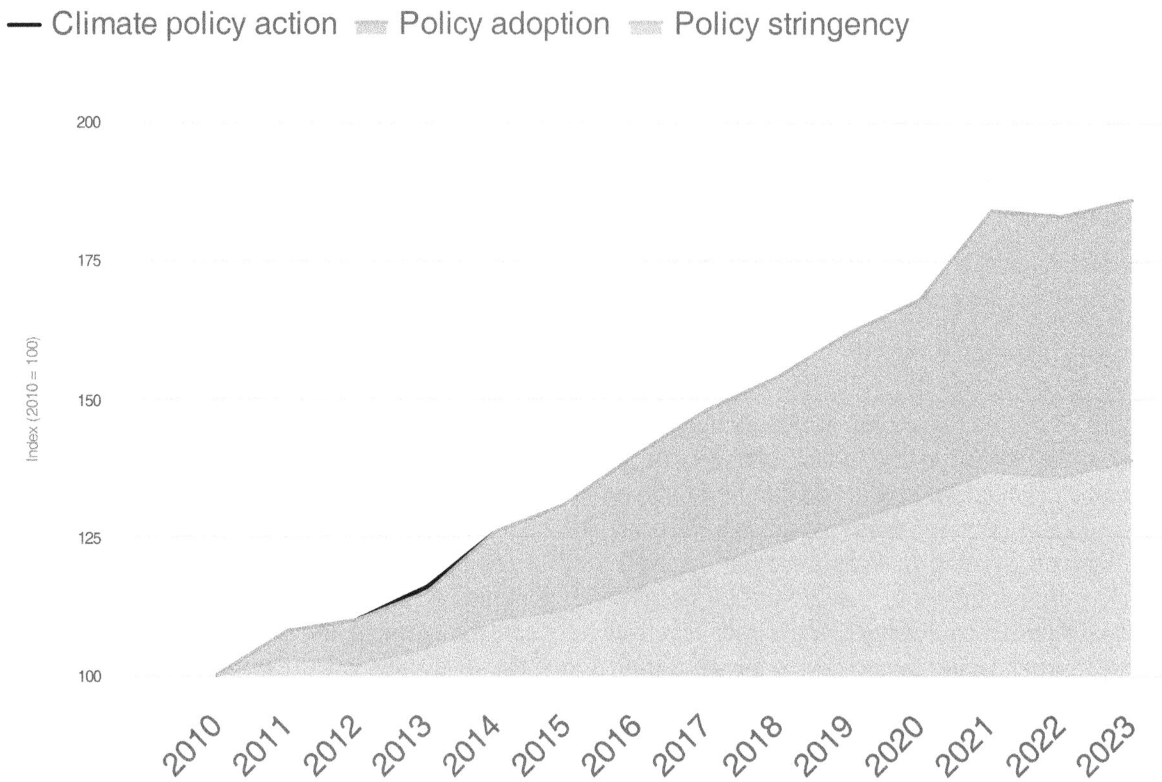

Note: Climate policy action is measured as a combination of policy adoption and policy stringency. See endnote 5 for details on the calculation of climate policy action.
Source: Based on data from OECD, IEA, ITF, World Bank and others using the methodology of Nachtigall et al. (2022): "The climate actions and policies measurement framework: A structured and harmonised climate policy database to monitor countries' mitigation action", *OECD Environment Working Papers*, No. 203, OECD Publishing, Paris, https://doi.org/10.1787/2caa60ce-en

The gap in climate policy action between OECD and OECD partner countries continued to widen

In 2023, climate policy action increased in 41 countries, accounting for around 60% of global GHG emissions. At the same time, it contracted in eight countries, accounting for 8% of GHG emissions. On average, OECD countries had stronger climate action in place than OECD partners; this trend has been progressively widening over time, increasing by almost 2% in 2023 (Figure 3.3). The increasing disparity of climate action between countries can affect competitiveness and may lead to carbon leakage, potentially undermining the effectiveness of increased climate action on global emissions reductions. This reinforces the need for enhanced international co-ordination and co-operation to ensure fulfilment of national commitments and achievement of global objectives.

Figure 3.3. The disparity in climate action between OECD countries and OECD partner countries is growing wider

Climate action (0-10) differentiated by OECD and OECD partner countries, 1990-2023

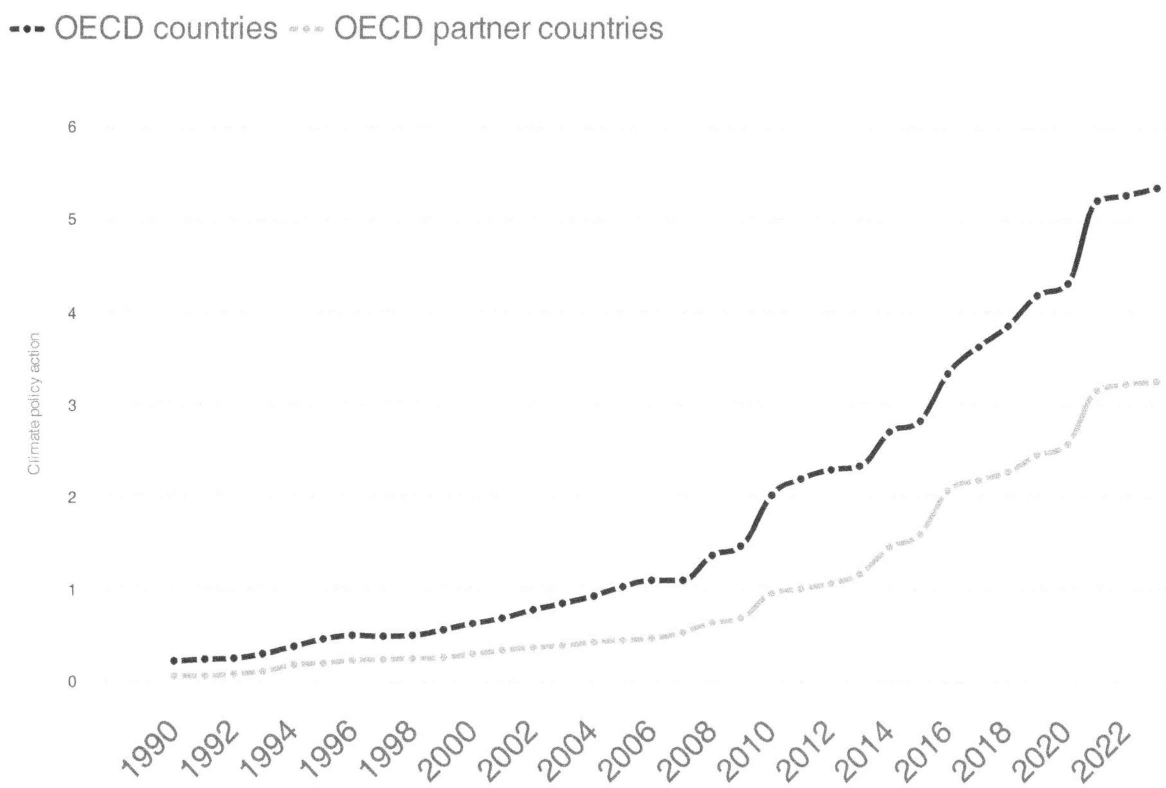

Note: The sharp increase in climate policy action in 2010 can be partly explained by a simultaneous improvement in data availability. For example, data on fossil fuel subsidy reform only became available from 2010. Climate policy action is measured as a combination of policy adoption and policy stringency. See endnote 5 for details on the calculation of climate policy action. Country group averages are calculated using an unweighted average across the respective countries.

Source: Based on data from OECD, IEA, ITF, World Bank and others using the methodology of Nachtigall et al. (2022): "The climate actions and policies measurement framework: A structured and harmonised climate policy database to monitor countries' mitigation action", OECD Environment Working Papers, No. 203, OECD Publishing, Paris, https://doi.org/10.1787/2caa60ce-en

Climate policy action of some sector-specific policies has picked up

Sectoral climate policy action picked-up in 2023. This was driven by increased policy action in the transport, buildings and industry sectors (Figure A.1.), steered by increased action of nMBIs (see below). Using the CAPMF data, a study led by the Potsdam Institute for Climate Impact Research indicates that certain sectoral policies were responsible for significant emissions reductions in various countries (Box 3.1).

In contrast, climate policy action in the electricity sector decreased, primarily due to fewer renewable energy auctions. The slowdown of climate policy action in the electricity sector is accompanied by a rise of electricity-related emissions. Despite more availability of cost-competitive renewables (IRENA, 2022[9]), electricity-related emissions in OECD and OECD partner countries grew by over 2% in 2022, remaining the major emissions source. On the positive side, more countries committed to coal bans and phase-outs.[6]

In 2023, countries continued the upward trend in international climate co-operation policies. This was primarily due to the improved provision of climate data, such as such as the implementation of the System of Economic and Environmental Accounts (UN, 2012[10]). Cross-sectoral policies also experienced some increases, due to improvements in fossil fuel production policies, public expenditure of research, development and demonstration, and setting climate targets. However, virtually no country accelerated net-zero target ambitions, which have increasingly become a source of domestic political contention (Nature, 2023[11]). (see Figure A.3 for more details).

Figure 3.4. Sector-specific policy efforts have picked-up

Climate policy action (0-10) by policy area, OECD and OECD partner countries, 2010-2023

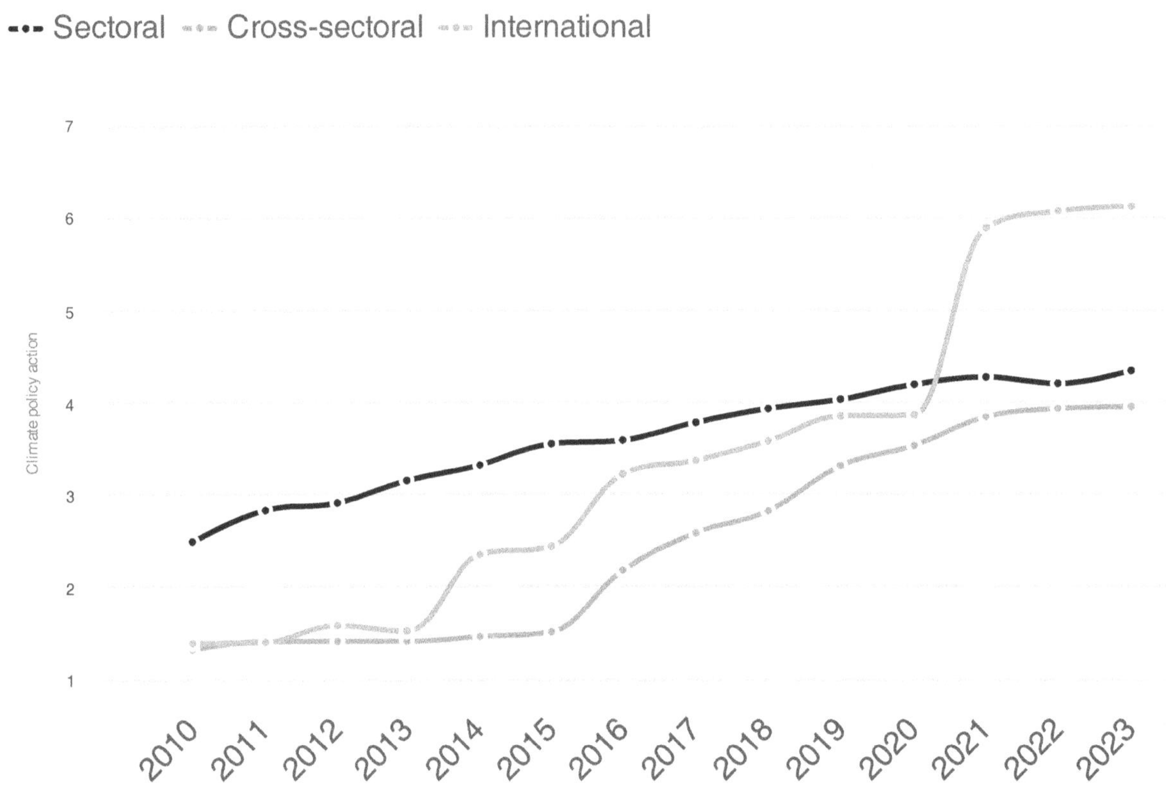

Note: Climate policy action is measured as a combination of policy adoption and policy stringency. See endnote 5 for details on the calculation of climate policy action.

Source: Based on data from OECD, IEA, ITF, World Bank and others using the methodology of Nachtigall, D. et al. (2022): "The climate actions and policies measurement framework: A structured and harmonised climate policy database to monitor countries' mitigation action", OECD Environment Working Papers, No. 203, OECD Publishing, Paris, https://doi.org/10.1787/2caa60ce-en

Box 3.1. Climate policies that have resulted in significant reductions in emissions

Policy makers, researchers and businesses need to know which policies reduce emissions at scale to meet the temperature goals of the Paris Agreement. A study led by the Potsdam Institute for Climate Impact Research combines the CAPMF data with a machine learning approach to detect major emissions breaks. This provides the first global, systematic *ex post* evaluation to identify policies and policy mixes that have led to large emissions reductions.

Figure 3.5 illustrates two detected emissions breaks (vertical red lines) in Great Britain's electricity sector. These follow the introduction of a carbon price floor (CPF) that imposed a minimum carbon price for power producers in the EU Emissions Trading System. The literature has attributed most of the decline in emissions to the CPF (Abrell, Kosch and Rausch, 2022[12]; Leroutier, 2022[13]; Döbbeling-Hildebrandt et al., 2024[14]). This study reveals the CPF was part of a wide policy mix, indicated by the coloured squares at the bottom of Figure 3.5. The mix highlighted the importance of non-market-based instruments such as renewable portfolio standards or stricter air pollution standards alongside market-based instruments such as feed-in-tariffs and auctions.

Figure 3.5. Policy mixes that led to substantial emissions reductions

Emissions and policy adoption or strengthening: Great Britain's electricity sector 2000-2022

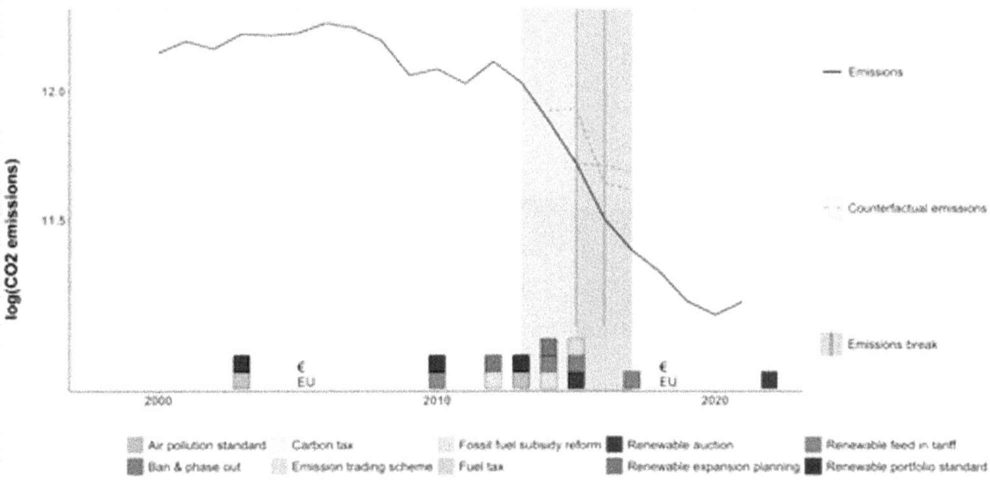

The study also offers a broad range of important findings and policy recommendations. Most identified emissions reductions were linked to two or more measures, highlighting the importance of policy mixes. There is no one-size fits all approach; successful policies and policy mixes vary across sectors and countries. Carbon pricing is particularly effective in the electricity and industry sector, both of which are characterised by firms that seek to maximise profit. Emissions reductions in the buildings and transport sectors – which are typically characterised by heterogeneous households – mostly require a complex mix of policies, including non-market-based instruments. Carbon pricing, regulation and subsidies work well in developed countries, but carbon pricing does not always work in developing countries. In developing countries, the study could not identify emissions breaks associated with carbon pricing in the transport and electricity sectors.

Source: (Stechemesser et al., 2024[6]).

Market-based instruments continued to decrease, non-market-based instruments increased and actions based on targets remained strong

Market-based instruments use continued to decrease

The use of MBIs has declined for the second consecutive year, primarily driven by reduced financial support for renewable electricity, notably auctions (Figure 3.6). This trend reflects both governments' diminishing fiscal space and reluctance to implement or strengthen carbon pricing schemes (Dechezleprêtre et al., 2022[15]). On a positive note, the European Union has passed the "Fit-for-55" package, which includes a plan to implement ETS II to cover the buildings, road and maritime transport sectors (European Commission, 2023[16]). However, as ETS II will only become fully operational by 2027, the CAPMF does not currently take it into account.[7]

Figure 3.6. Market-based instruments declined due to reductions in environmentally beneficial subsidies

Climate policy action (0-10) of market-based instruments by type: OECD and OECD partner countries, 2010-2023

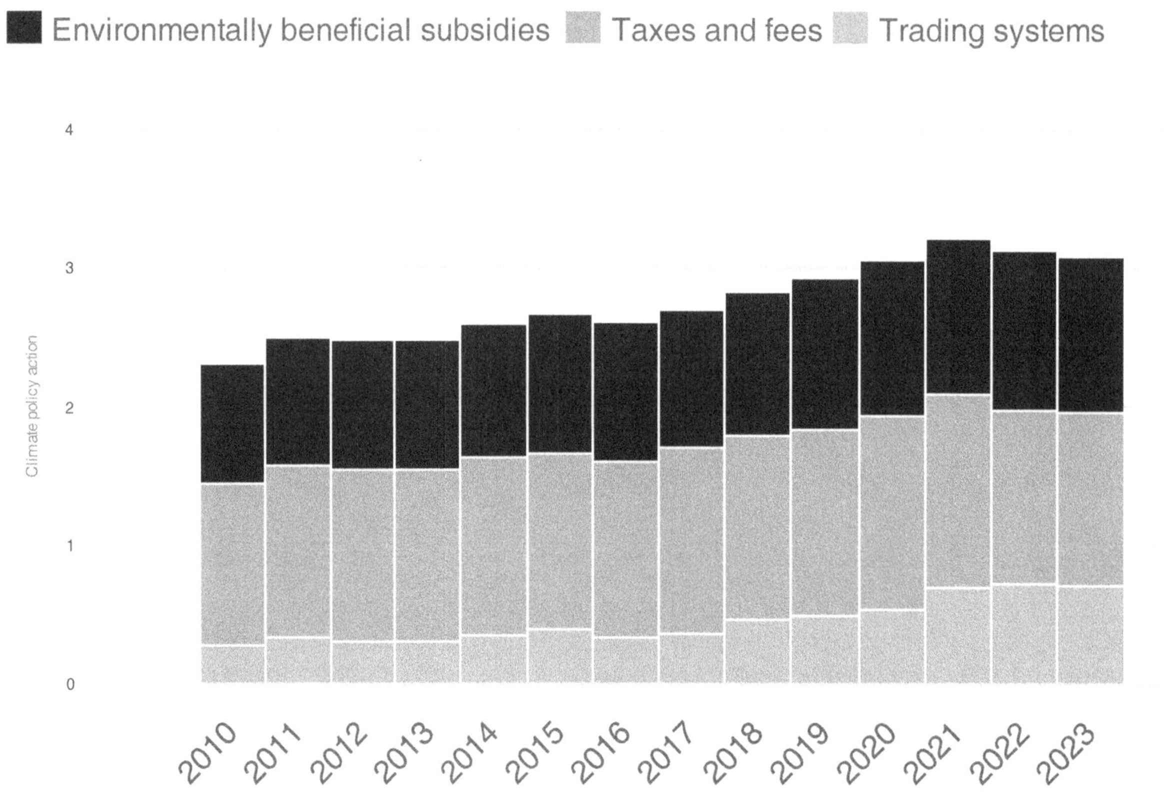

Note: Climate policy action is measured as a combination of policy adoption and policy stringency. See endnote 5 for details on the calculation of climate policy action.
Source: Based on data from OECD, IEA, ITF, World Bank and others using the methodology of Nachtigall, D. et al. (2022): "The climate actions and policies measurement framework: A structured and harmonised climate policy database to monitor countries' mitigation action", *OECD Environment Working Papers,* No. 203, OECD Publishing, Paris, https://doi.org/10.1787/2caa60ce-en

Non-market-based instruments are growing driven by performance standards

In contrast to MBIs, the use of nMBIs increased sharply in 2023 (Figure 3.7). This was primarily due to more stringent performance standards, notably related to EU minimum energy performance standards (MEPS) for electric motors. There was also some progress in other performance standards, technology standards and information instruments. For example, Peru adopted new MEPS for appliances, and the European Union banned the sale of new passenger cars with internal combustion engines by 2035.

Figure 3.7. Non-market-based instruments benefited significantly from stronger performance standards

Climate policy action (0-10) of non-market-based instruments by type, OECD and OECD partner countries, 2010-2023

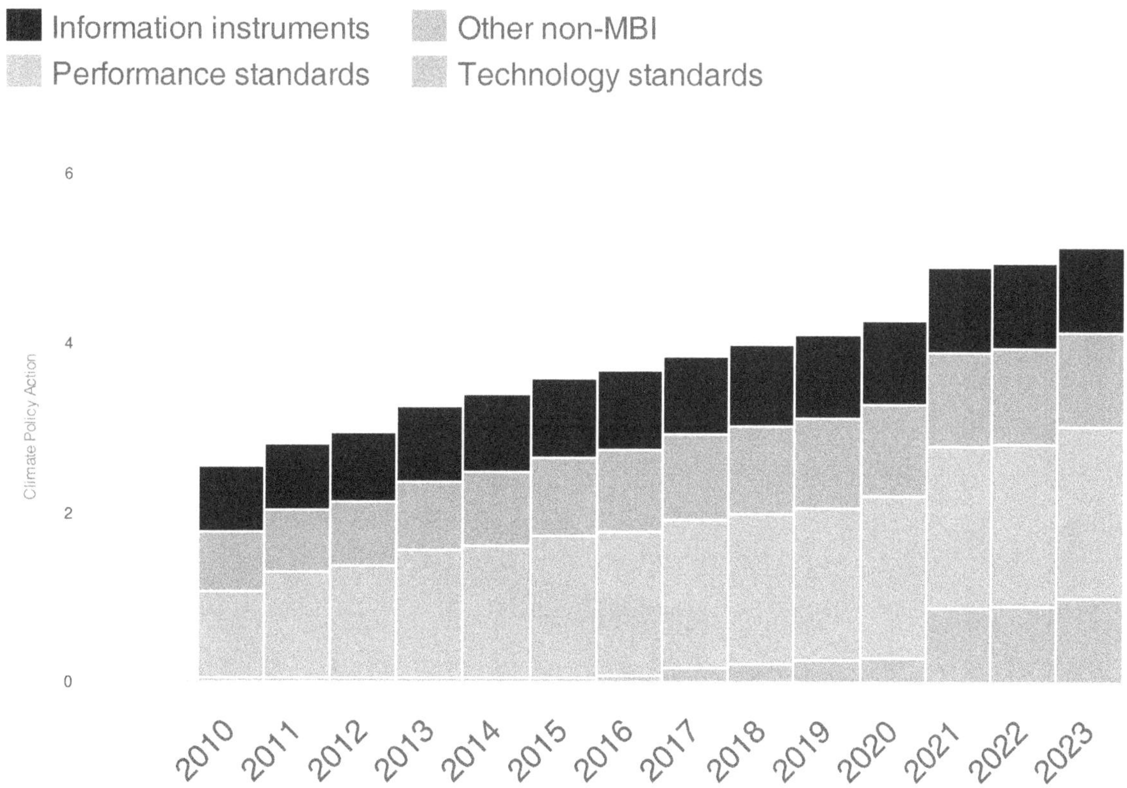

Note: Climate policy action is measured as a combination of policy adoption and policy stringency. See endnote 5 for details on the calculation of climate policy action.
Source: Based on data from OECD, IEA, ITF, World Bank and others using the methodology of Nachtigall, D. et al. (2022): "The climate actions and policies measurement framework: A structured and harmonised climate policy database to monitor countries' mitigation action", *OECD Environment Working Papers,* No. 203, OECD Publishing, Paris, https://doi.org/10.1787/2caa60ce-en

Countries advanced on policies related to setting targets, governance, climate data provision and international co-operation

Policy actions related to targets, governance, climate data and international co-operation increased slightly after having grown significantly with adoption of the Paris Agreement in 2015 (Figure 3.8). Positive developments in 2023 include Korea's ratification of the Kigali Amendment to reduce the consumption and production of hydrofluorocarbons (HFCs) (UNEP, 2022[17]). In addition, countries such as Iceland, Ireland and France significantly ramped up financing of their climate advisory bodies, highlighting their importance to guide and advise governments, and ensure commitment and accountability. Developed countries exceeded the USD 100 billion goal of climate finance for the first time in 2022, reaching USD 115.9 billion (OECD, 2024[18]).[8]

Figure 3.8. Countries slightly advanced on policies related to targets, governance, climate data and international co-operation

Climate policy action (0-10) of climate policies by type, OECD and OECD partner countries, 2010-2023

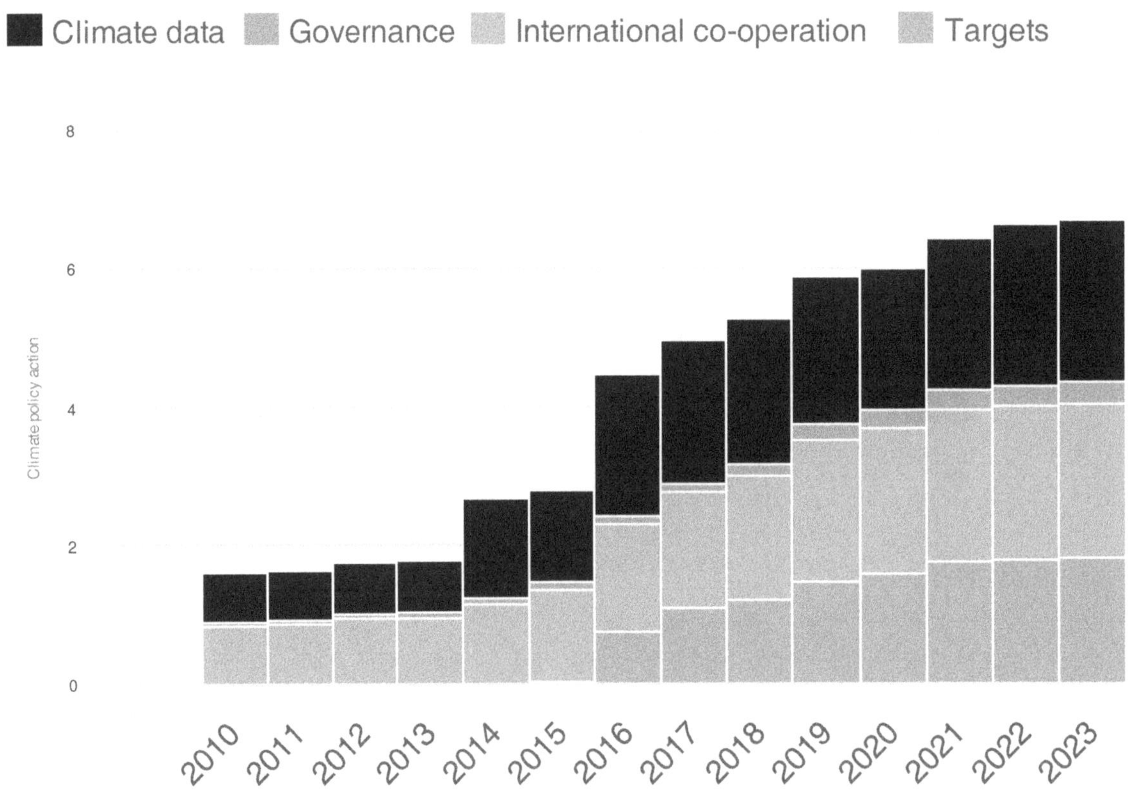

Source: Based on data from OECD, IEA, ITF, World Bank and others using the methodology of Nachtigall, D. et al. (2022): "The climate actions and policies measurement framework: A structured and harmonised climate policy database to monitor countries' mitigation action", *OECD Environment Working Papers*, No. 203, OECD Publishing, Paris, https://doi.org/10.1787/2caa60ce-en

Countries use different policy mix to meet their emissions reduction targets

The climate change policy mix can be broadly defined as governments' general strategy to reduce emissions through adoption of different types and stringency levels of policies tailored to different emissions sources. While the CAPMF cannot capture the entire complexity of countries' policy approaches, it can identify key characteristics. These include the number of adopted policies, the stringency, the types (e.g. MBIs versus nMBIs), and the sectoral focus.

This section presents different characteristics of countries' policy mix, contrasting OECD with OECD partner countries in the year 2023. More details on the heterogeneity of policy approaches across countries, along with detailed country-level data, can be found in the IPAC Dashboard.

The climate policy mix results from a complex interaction between past climate action, climate ambitions, emissions profiles and available technologies, as well as countries' cultural, social, political and institutional conditions, among other factors. There is no one-size-fits-all policy approach and no single recipe for effectiveness. Assessing policy effectiveness requires more sophisticated econometric or modelling techniques, such as those presented in Box 3.1 or proposed under the OECD Inclusive Forum on Carbon Mitigation Approaches (IFCMA) (OECD, 2023[19]).

OECD countries have more policies than partner countries do, but their stringency levels are comparable

OECD countries, on average, have a higher policy density than OECD partners have, while the levels of stringency are comparable (Figure 3.9). OECD countries generally use a more complex mix of policies to reduce emissions. This difference also explains the divergence of climate action between OECD and OECD partner countries in 2023. Since OECD countries had adopted more policies and most of their increased climate policy action was driven by strengthening existing policies, their climate policy action expanded more than those of OECD partner countries.

OECD partner countries have less stringent policies, though some countries reach stringency levels of OECD countries (Figure 3.9, lower panel). The CAPMF data illustrate that some countries prefer to adopt relatively few, albeit stringent, policies. Conversely, others prefer to adopt many policies with rather low stringency. Both approaches culminate in the same level of overall climate policy action. Using CAPMF data, a recent OECD study sheds light on the heterogeneity of countries' mitigation strategies (D'Arcangelo, Kruse and Pisu, 2023[5]). Its findings suggest that strategies with more diverse policy instruments may create synergies that enable countries to reduce emissions at a lower level of policy stringency than introducing few instruments.

Figure 3.9. Difference in climate policy action between OECD countries and partners is mostly driven by differences in policy density, not policy stringency

Policy adoption and average stringency of adopted policies by country group: 2023

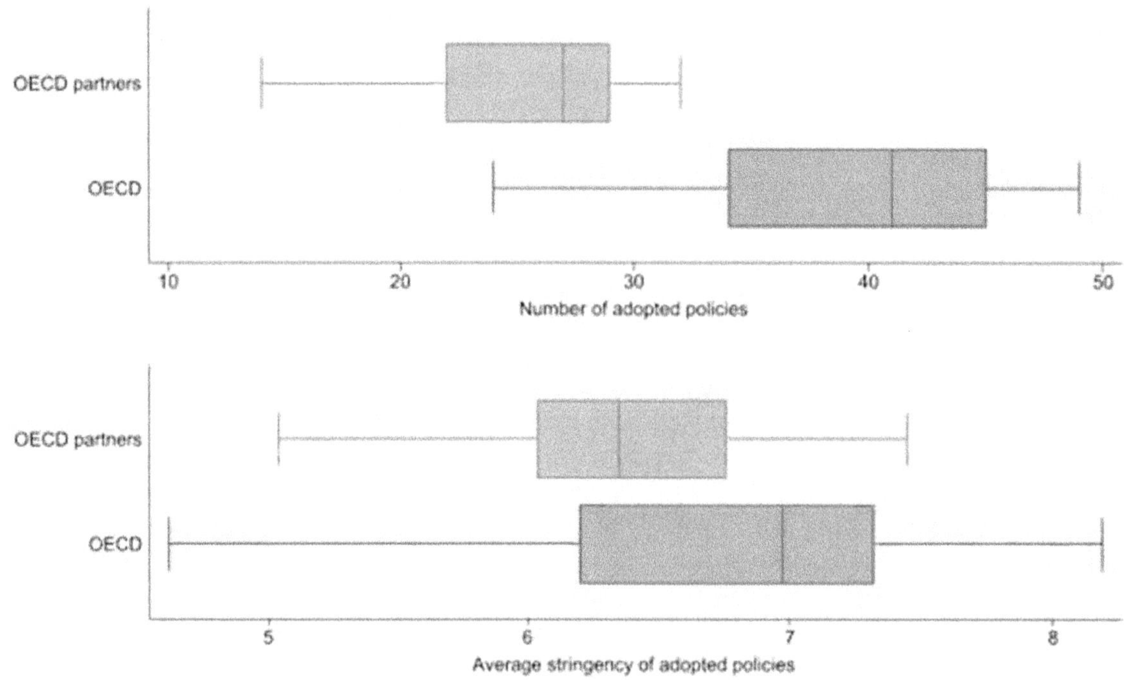

Source: Based on data from OECD, IEA, ITF, World Bank and others using the methodology of Nachtigall et al. (2022): "The climate actions and policies measurement framework: A structured and harmonised climate policy database to monitor countries' mitigation action", *OECD Environment Working Papers*, No. 203, OECD Publishing, Paris, https://doi.org/10.1787/2caa60ce-en.

OECD partner countries place a greater emphasis on non-market-based instruments

OECD partner countries put much more emphasis on the use of nMBIs compared to OECD countries (Figure 3.10). For instance, information instruments – one type of nMBI – in OECD partner countries exceeds that in OECD countries (Figure A.8). Climate policy actions related to targets, governance, climate data and international co-operation also play a larger role in OECD partner countries whereas MBIs are more used in OECD countries.

Figure 3.10. Non-market-based instruments are more prevalent in OECD partner countries

Share of climate policy action by policy type and country group, 2023

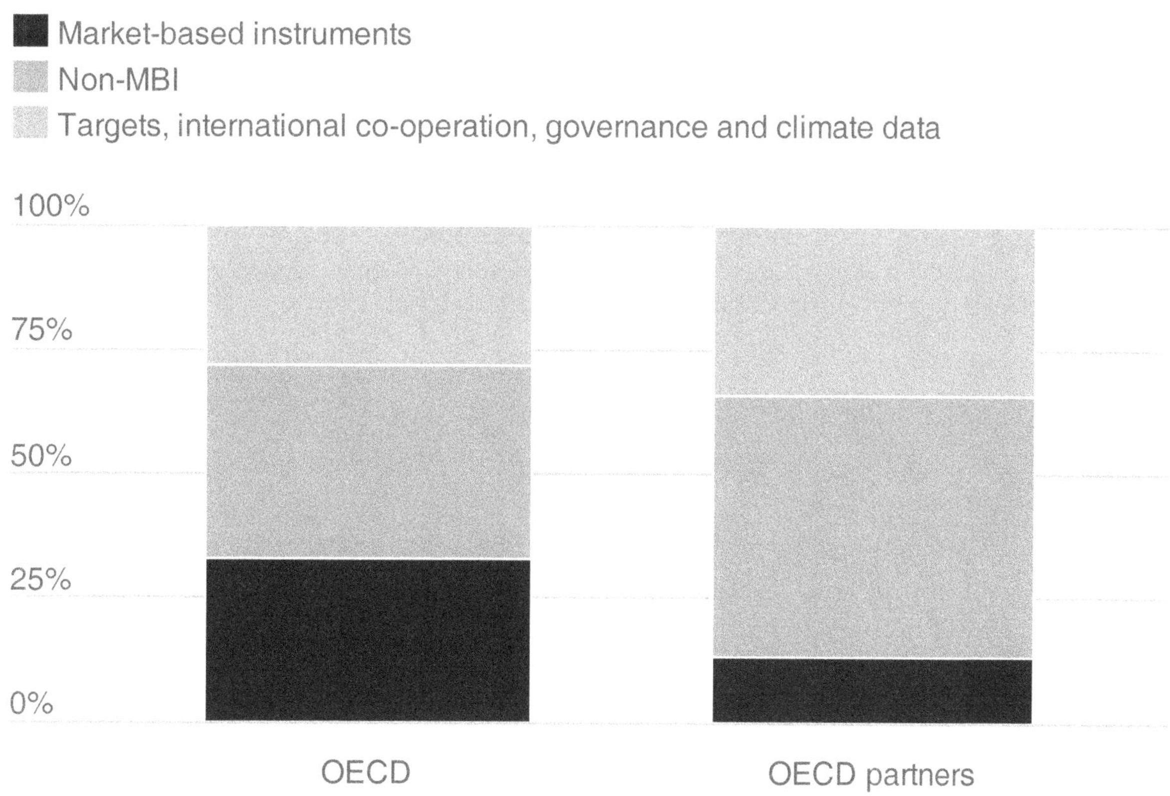

Note: Climate policy action is measured as a combination of policy adoption and policy stringency. See endnote 5 for details on the calculation of climate policy action.

Source: Based on data from OECD, IEA, ITF, World Bank and others using the methodology of Nachtigall, D. et al. (2022): "The climate actions and policies measurement framework: A structured and harmonised climate policy database to monitor countries' mitigation action", *OECD Environment Working Papers*, No. 203, OECD Publishing, Paris, https://doi.org/10.1787/2caa60ce-en

The predominance of nMBIs in OECD partner countries may reflect, among other reasons, the lower administrative capacity to adopt and enforce the policies compared to MBIs.[9] Some OECD partner countries may lack administrative capacity to administer complex MBIs such as an ETS (Narassimhan et al., 2018[20]). Partner countries may also prefer to use their budget for other purposes than to subsidise the development and deployment of low-carbon technologies – a key MBI. The prevalent use of nMBIs in OECD partner countries' policy mix reiterates the importance of describing them. Without this information, policymakers, researchers and businesses would misinterpret the climate policy action of OECD partner countries.

Climate action is misaligned with countries' emissions profile in transport and electricity sectors

The descriptive analysis suggests that climate policy action may not be well-aligned across emission source sectors. Across the four sectors covered by the CAPMF, transport accounts for the highest share of energy-related emissions in OECD countries, but climate action is second to lowest (Figure 3.11). Similarly, in OECD partner countries, climate action in the electricity sector is the lowest, yet this sector accounts for the largest share of emissions (Figure 3.11). The building sector in both OECD and OECD partner countries shows high levels of climate action, but its share of emissions is lowest in both country groups.

The apparent misalignment of the level of climate policy action and GHG emissions across different sectors suggests possible avenues for more effective climate action. Although there are many other considerations, such as effectiveness, equity and costs, these, albeit indicative, results would suggest that OECD countries need to intensify climate policy action in the transport sector while OECD partner countries need to focus action on the electricity sector. In the first case, some countries have implemented new policies. For example, countries are increasingly channeling funds towards electric mobility whereas the European Union expanded its emissions trading scheme towards the transport (and buildings) sectors. In the second case, more needs to be done to decarbonise the electricity sector. While the CAPMF can provide a first indication of a potential misalignment, more work is needed to assess countries' specific conditions and restrictions to provide tailored policy recommendations.

Figure 3.11. OECD countries need to intensify climate action in the transport sector

Climate policy action and share of emissions by sector: OECD countries, 2023

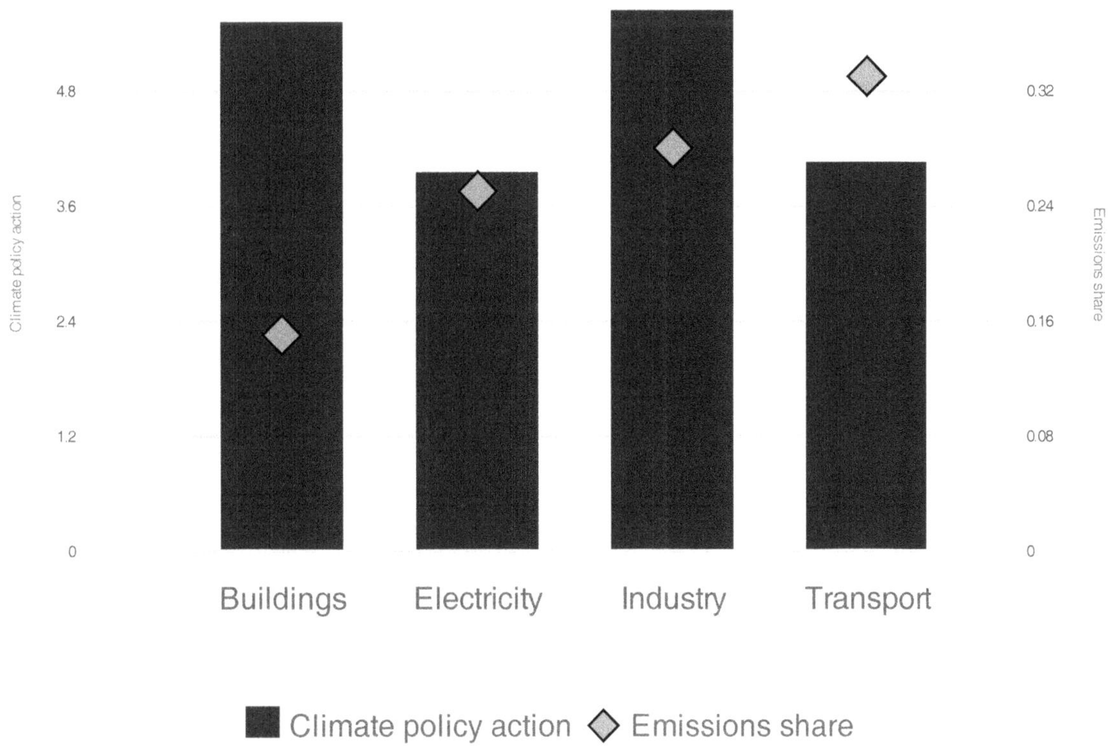

Note: Climate policy action is measured as a combination of policy adoption and policy stringency. See endnote 5 for details on the calculation of climate policy action.
Source: Based on data from OECD, IEA, ITF, World Bank and others using the methodology of Nachtigall, D. et al. (2022): "The climate actions and policies measurement framework: A structured and harmonised climate policy database to monitor countries' mitigation action", *OECD Environment Working Papers*, No. 203, OECD Publishing, Paris, https://doi.org/10.1787/2caa60ce-en. Emissions data are from European Commission, Joint Research Centre (JRC)/Netherlands Environmental Assessment Agency (PBL): Emission Database for Global Atmospheric Research (EDGAR).

Figure 3.12. OECD partner countries could intensify climate action in the electricity sector

Climate policy action and share of emissions by sector: OECD partner countries, 2023

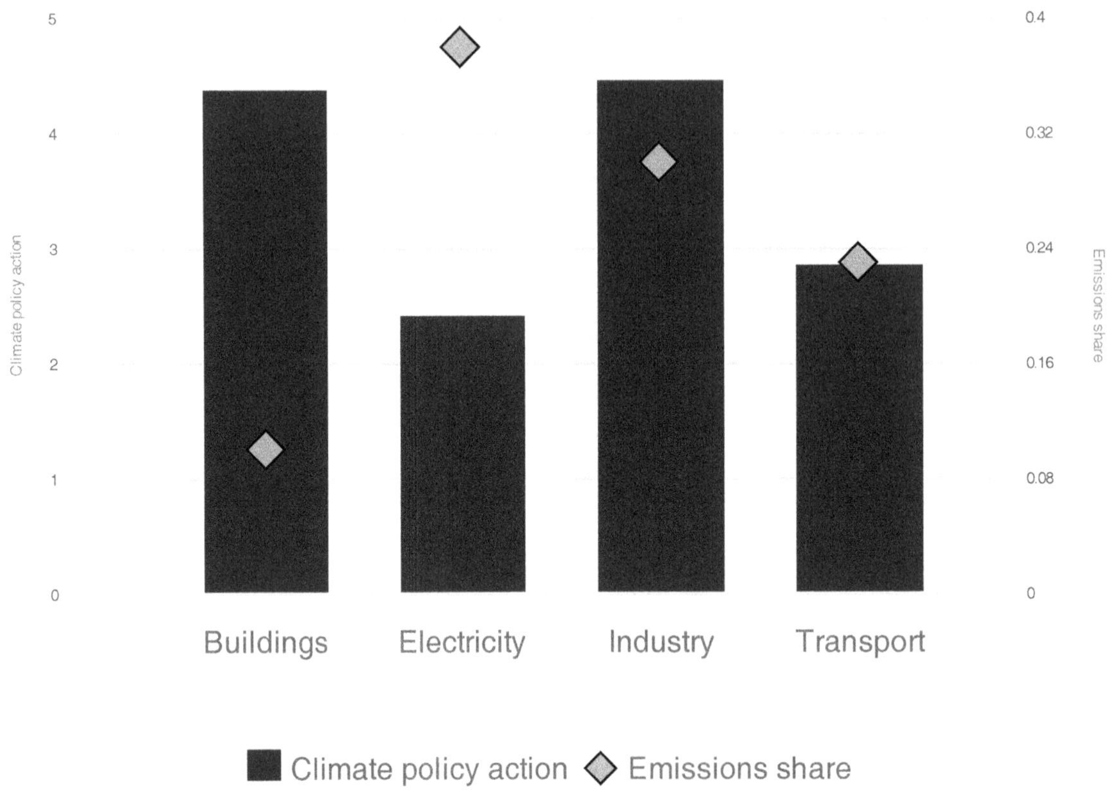

Note: Based on data from OECD, IEA, ITF, World Bank and others using the methodology of Nachtigall, D. et al. (2022): "The climate actions and policies measurement framework: A structured and harmonised climate policy database to monitor countries' mitigation action", *OECD Environment Working Papers*, No. 203, OECD Publishing, Paris, https://doi.org/10.1787/2caa60ce-en. Emissions data are from European Commission, Joint Research Centre (JRC)/Netherlands Environmental Assessment Agency (PBL): Emission Database for Global Atmospheric Research (EDGAR).

Climate adaptation is increasingly becoming a priority for countries

In recent years, climate adaptation has emerged as a top priority for countries, driven by the escalating impacts of climate-related hazards (Chapter 2). Tracking adaptation policies could further support stakeholder engagement, promote peer learning and raise the efficacy of adaptation initiatives. Some progress has been made in surveying adaptation policies (OECD, 2024[21]), however more work needs to be done to identify a set of indicators that can better reflect each country's specific climate-risk profile.

The number of countries submitting National Adaptation Plans (NAPs) and National Adaptation Communications to the United Nations Framework Convention on Climate Change (UNFCCC) provides an indicator of the expansion of climate adaptation efforts. The metric serves as a crucial indicator for assessing climate action under the Sustainable Development Goals (SDGs) (UN, 2017[22]). NAPs have surged since the adoption of the Paris Agreement to more than 50 countries in 2023 (Figure 3.13). This indicator provides a first glance of countries' priorities and strategies for climate adaptation. However, it needs to be underpinned by concrete actions and robust monitoring frameworks to be effective.

Figure 3.13. Countries are increasingly adopting key adaption plans and strategies

Number of countries that submitted adaptation documents to the UNFCCC: All countries, 2010-2023

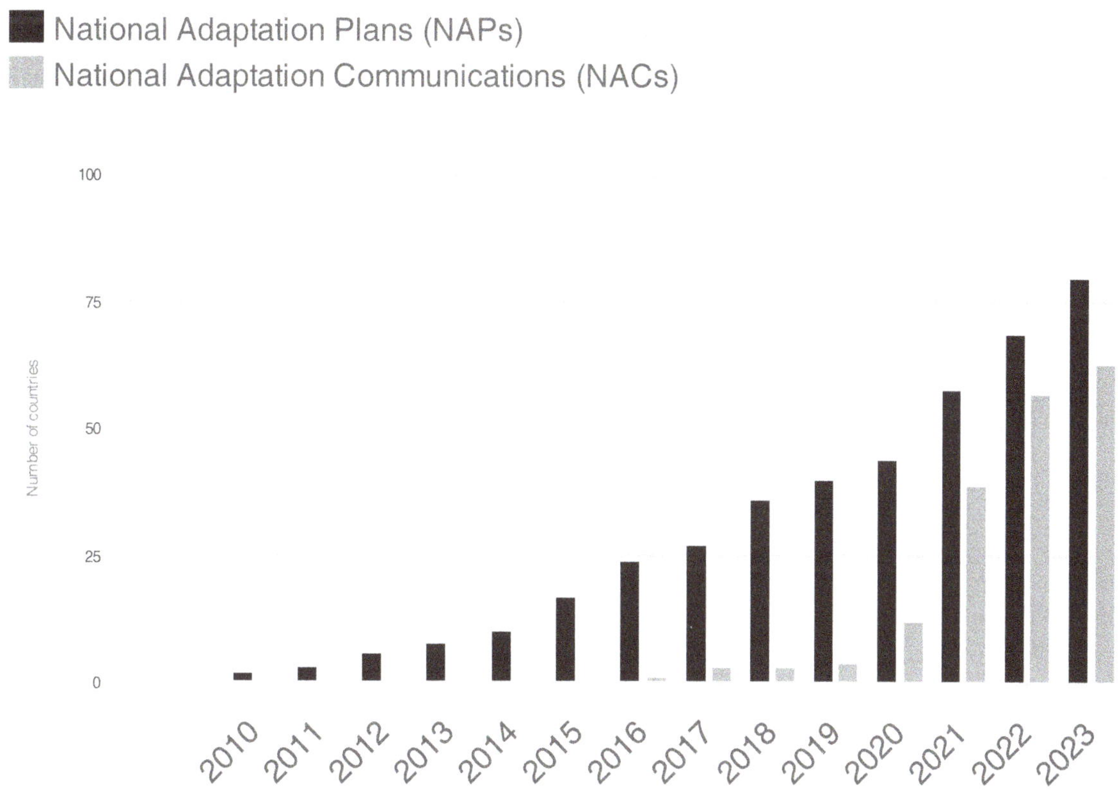

Source: OECD (2024), "Measuring progress in implementing national adaptation policies", in *Measuring Progress in Adapting to a Changing Climate: Insights from OECD countries*, OECD Publishing, Paris, https://doi.org/10.1787/7035bc15-en; UNFCCC Adaptation Communication Registry and NAP central.

Climate action and enhanced ambition

Climate-related hazards have reached unprecedented levels. Yet, under current policies, global GHG emissions are projected to rise by 2030 (UNEP, 2024[23]). While many countries have expanded their climate policy action efforts in recent decades, there is a critical need to enhance ambition and align action with the temperature goals set by the Paris Agreement.

Consistent with other international reports such as the UNEP emissions gap report (UNEP, 2023[24]) (UNEP, 2024[23]), the 2024 edition of the Climate Action Monitor confirms that current NDCs fall short of the GHG emission reductions necessary to achieve the Paris Agreement goals, creating an ambition gap. Moreover, current climate policies are insufficient to meet countries' NDCs, as pointed out in the Global Stocktake (UNFCCC, 2023[1]). The Sixth Assessment Report of the Intergovernmental Panel on Climate Change estimated that policies implemented by the end of 2020 are projected to result in higher global greenhouse gas emissions than even the modest emission reduction commitments presented in NDCs, indicating an implementation gap. The slow progress of climate policy action in 2022 and 2023, as reported in this Monitor, poses a risk of countries failing to close the implementation gap.

Nevertheless, there are considerable opportunities for countries to address and narrow the implementation and ambition gaps. The upcoming submissions of new NDCs by early 2025 presents a crucial moment at COP29 to boost ambition and work towards limiting global warming to 1.5°C. More ambitious NDCs must be underpinned by concrete climate actions and policy instruments to effectively reduce emissions and close the implementation gap. Tracking trends in climate action is therefore essential for assessing countries' efforts. Databases that track climate policy action can play a pivotal role in uncovering key policy trends by providing extensive information on the adoption and stringency of selected climate mitigation policies.

Improving policy data is essential to better support countries in reaching their emissions targets. The OECD's Horizontal Project Net Zero+, which explores how governments can enhance climate and economic resilience, and IPAC which collects foundational data and develops key indicators, can support countries by providing key information and evidence-based policy recommendations. These complementary efforts are vital to provide a comprehensive overview of countries' mitigation policy landscape and will support policy makers in implementing better climate policies for better lives.

References

Abrell, J., M. Kosch and S. Rausch (2022), "How effective is carbon pricing? A machine learning approach to policy evaluation", *Journal of Environmental Economics and Management*, Vol. 112, p. 102589, https://doi.org/10.1016/j.jeem.2021.102589. [12]

COP28 UAE (2023), "Global Renewables and Energy Efficiency Pledge (COP28)", webpage, https://www.cop28.com/en/global-renewables-and-energy-efficiency-pledge (accessed on 15 August 2024). [4]

D'Arcangelo, F., T. Kruse and M. Pisu (2023), "Identifying and tracking climate change mitigation strategies: A cluster-based assessment", *OECD Economics Department Working Papers*, No. 1786, OECD Publishing, Paris, https://doi.org/10.1787/a23b43c5-en. [5]

Dechezleprêtre, A. et al. (2022), "Fighting climate change: International attitudes toward climate policies", *OECD Economics Department Working Papers*, No. 1714, OECD Publishing, Paris, https://doi.org/10.1787/3406f29a-en. [15]

Döbbeling-Hildebrandt, N. et al. (2024), "Systematic review and meta-analysis of ex-post evaluations on the effectiveness of carbon pricing", *Nature Communications*, Vol. 15/1, https://doi.org/10.1038/s41467-024-48512-w. [14]

European Commission (2023), "ETS2: Buildings, Road Transport and Additional Sectors", webpage, https://climate.ec.europa.eu/eu-action/eu-emissions-trading-system-eu-ets/ets2-buildings-road-transport-and-additional-sectors_en (accessed on 15 August 2024). [16]

IPCC (2022), *IPCC Sixth Assessment Report Working Group III: Mitigation of Climate Change*, Intergovernmental Panel on Climate Change, Geneva, https://www.ipcc.ch/report/ar6/wg3/. [3]

IRENA (2022), *Renewable Power Generation Costs in 2021*, International Renewable Energy Agency, Abu Dhabi. [9]

Kruse, T. et al. (2022), "Measuring environmental policy stringency in OECD countries: An update of the OECD composite EPS indicator", *OECD Economics Department Working Papers*, No. 1703, OECD Publishing, Paris, https://doi.org/10.1787/90ab82e8-en. [25]

Leroutier, M. (2022), “Carbon pricing and power sector decarbonization: Evidence from the UK”, *Journal of Environmental Economics and Management*, Vol. 111, p. 102580, https://doi.org/10.1016/j.jeem.2021.102580. [13]

Nachtigall, D. et al. (2024), “The climate actions and policies measurement framework: A database to monitor and assess countries’ mitigation action”, *Environmental and Resource Economics*, Vol. 87/1, pp. 191-217, https://doi.org/10.1007/s10640-023-00821-2. [8]

Nachtigall, D. et al. (2022), “The climate actions and policies measurement framework: A structured and harmonised climate policy database to monitor countries’ mitigation action”, *OECD Environment Working Papers*, No. 203, OECD Publishing, Paris, https://doi.org/10.1787/2caa60ce-en. [2]

Narassimhan, E. et al. (2018), “Carbon pricing in practice: A review of existing emissions trading systems”, *Climate Policy*, Vol. 18/8, pp. 967-991, https://doi.org/10.1080/14693062.2018.1467827. [20]

Nature, E. (2023), “Shock delay to net-zero pledges turns UK from climate leader to laggard”, *Nature*, Vol. 621/7980, pp. 657-658, https://doi.org/10.1038/d41586-023-02987-7. [11]

OECD (2024), *Climate Finance Provided and Mobilised by Developed Countries in 2013-2022*, Climate Finance and the USD 100 Billion Goal, OECD Publishing, Paris, https://doi.org/10.1787/19150727-en. [18]

OECD (2024), *Measuring Progress in Adapting to a Changing Climate: Insights from OECD countries*, OECD Publishing, Paris, https://doi.org/10.1787/8cfe45af-en. [21]

OECD (2023), “Inclusive Forum on Carbon Mitigation Approaches (IFCMA)”, webpage, https://www.oecd.org/en/about/programmes/inclusive-forum-on-carbon-mitigation-approaches.html (accessed on 15 August 2024). [19]

OECD (2023), *The Climate Action Monitor 2023: Providing Information to Monitor Progress Towards Net-Zero*, OECD Publishing, Paris, https://doi.org/10.1787/60e338a2-en. [7]

PPCA (2017), *Powering Past Coal Alliance Declaration*, https://poweringpastcoal.org/declaration/. [26]

Stechemesser, A. et al. (2024), “Climate policies that achieved major emission reductions: Global evidence from two decades”, *Science*, Vol. 385/6711, pp. 884-892, https://doi.org/10.1126/science.adl6547. [6]

UN (2017), “Global Indicator Framework for the Sustainable Development Goals and Targets of the 2030 Agenda for Sustainable Development”, *Report of the Inter-Agency and Expert Group on Sustainable Development Goal Indicators (E/CN.3/2017/2) - Annex III*, United Nations Statistics Division, https://unstats.un.org/sdgs/indicators/indicators-list/. [22]

UN (2012), *System of Environmental-Economic Accounting 2012: Central Framework*, United Nations Statistics Division, New York, https://unstats.un.org/unsd/envaccounting/seeaRev/SEEA_CF_Final_en.pdf. [10]

UNEP (2024), *Emissions Gap Report 2024: No more hot air … please! With a massive gap between rhetoric and reality, countries draft new climate commitments*, https://www.unep.org/emissions-gap-report-2024. [23]

UNEP (2023), *Emissions Gap Report 2023: Broken Record – Temperatures hit new highs, yet world fails to cut emissions (again)*, United Nations Environment Programme, https://doi.org/10.59117/20.500.11822/43922. [24]

UNEP (2022), "About Montreal Protocol", webpage, https://www.unep.org/ozonaction/who-we-are/about-montreal-protocol (accessed on 15 August 2024). [17]

UNFCCC (2023), *Outcome of the First Global Stocktake*, Fccc/Pa/Cma/2023/L.17, United Nations Framework Convention on Climate Change Secretariat, https://unfccc.int/sites/default/files/resource/cma2023_L17_adv.pdf. [1]

Notes

[1] In the Paris Agreement, Parties agreed to carry out every five years a global stocktake of implementation to assess collective progress towards achieving its goals.

[2] The CAPMF is a climate mitigation policy tracker and database that covers countries responsible for 63% of global GHG emissions. The CAPMF tracks 130 policy variables, grouped into 56 climate actions and policies, consistently from 1990 to 2023 across 50 countries and the EU-27 as a bloc. The United States has chosen to not include their data in CAPMF given concerns that CAPMF does not fully or accurately capture U.S. climate action.

[3] Policy stringency is defined as the degree to which policies incentivise emissions reductions. Following the methodology of the OECD Environmental Policy Stringency Index (Kruse et al., 2022[25]), the CAPMF calculates stringency as a relative concept by assigning a stringency score between 0 (not stringent) and 10 (very stringent) to each policy variable. This is based on the in-sample distribution across all countries and years of the policy variables' level (e.g. tax rate, emissions limit value, government expenditure) (Nachtigall et al., 2022[2]). High stringency values in a particular country do not necessarily suggest the policy is stringent enough to meet its mitigation goals. Rather, it means the policy in this country and year was more stringent compared to all other countries and years.

[4] The CAPMF should not be used as a performance indicator to rank countries' climate action as its policy scope may not represent adequately the policy approach of some countries. For example, information is limited in sectors such as agriculture, forestry and land use, as well as on specific instruments such as tax credits. Furthermore, the CAPMF does not fully capture new innovative instruments or climate actions such as carbon abatement payment or pledges (e.g. Global Renewables and Energy Efficiency Pledge) (COP28 UAE, 2023[4]) nor does it include the ETS II, which will only become fully operational in 2027. Thus, policies included in the CAPMF may not be fully representative of the mitigation approaches of some countries. In terms of interpretation, although previous work has found a positive association between climate action as measured by the CAPMF and emissions reductions (Nachtigall et al., 2024[8]), increasing climate policy action does not necessarily imply a stronger mitigation effect. The effects of increased policy adoption and policy stringency will depend on many factors such as emissions coverage and abatement costs and will likely have different impacts across countries depending on their emission profile, available energy resources, and institutional framework (Nachtigall et al., 2022[2]).

[5] The CAPMF calculates climate policy action as the average of policy stringency across all building blocks (sectoral, cross-sectoral, international policies). Policy stringency in each building block is calculated as

the average across all underlying modules (e.g. electricity market-based instruments, electricity non-market-based instruments), which – in turn – are calculated as the average of all policies included in each module. See Figure 2.1 in the methodological paper for the structure of the CAPMF (Nachtigall et al., 2022[2]). This approach is less subject to data availability compared to the unweighted average across all policies covered by the CAPMF. For some modules (e.g. electricity market-based instruments), the CAPMF comprises a large number of policies whereas for others (e.g. industry non- market-based instruments) it comprises only a few. Creating an unweighted average across all policies would, thus, bias overall climate action towards policy areas for which data availability is better. For the calculation of climate policy action of market-based or non market-based instruments, however, the CAPMF uses the unweighted average of policy stringency across all policies covered in the respective policy instrument type.

[6] For example, a number of countries joined the Powering Past Coal Alliance, which commits to accelerate the transition from unabated coal to clean energy (PPCA, 2017[26]). New members include the United States – the world's third largest coal user after China and India – as well as Colombia, the world's sixth largest coal exporter.

[7] Numbers in this report do not yet include country-level data estimates on fossil fuel subsidies (FFS) for 2023. Accounting for FFS data may turn the decline of climate policy action in MBIs to a slight increase. In fact, FFS introduced in 2022 to shield households and firms from rocketing energy prices as a result of the energy crisis were responsible for the decline of climate policy action in MBIs in 2022. However, FFS declined sharply in 2023 thanks to a decrease of the global oil price and to governments increasingly removing financial support for energy products (Figure A4).

[8] This milestone was reached but two years later than the original 2020 target year. Most of the growth in climate finance, compared to the previous year, can be attributed to bilateral and multilateral public finance, as well as to attributed private finance. The CAPMF does not capture international climate finance flows.

[9] In fact, some OECD partner countries such as China adopted MEPS for electric motors earlier than the European Union (Figure A5).

Annex A. Data gaps, methodology and limitations

Chapter 1

GHG emissions estimates

Official country-level data are based on emissions inventories reported to the United Nations Framework Convention on Climate Change (UNFCCC). These inventory data are compiled using territory-based and production-based principles following the Intergovernmental Panel on Climate Change (IPCC) guidelines. Since data are not available for all countries or all years, missing data are estimated to determine global aggregates for some countries. The data sources and methodology used in this publication are summarised below:

- GHG emissions data from national inventories are available for all OECD countries that report annually to UNFCCC for the period 1990-2022 (i.e. all Annex 1 countries and South Korea).
- Data for other OECD countries (formerly referred to as "non-Annex 1") are obtained through the OECD GHG emissions questionnaire. However, the time coverage is not complete. For example, Colombia covers data up to 2018, Costa Rica up to 2017 and Mexico up to 2019. There are also gaps for Israel before 2002.
- For OECD partner countries, many gaps remain. For example, official emissions data for 2020 are not available on the UNFCCC GHG emissions data interface. Major gaps are also present for large emitters, such as the People's Republic of China (hereafter "China") and India. China has provided official data for only five years (1994, 2005, 2010, 2012 and 2014), while India has presented data for only four years (1994, 2000, 2010 and 2016). There are also important gaps for Peru (for 1990-2010), Saudi Arabia (presenting only four years between 1990 and 2012), South Africa (for 1990-2000) and Indonesia (for 1990-2000).[1]
- In this report, when official data were not available, estimated data are used to compile global aggregates.

To deal with data gaps, the OECD developed a methodology to impute missing values in a consistent manner maintaining coherence with official reports (Cardenas et al, 2024). The methodology uses PRIMAP-hist national historical emissions time series adjusted to official estimates to impute values. The methodology is as follows:

- If all official series are missing, the PRIMAP series is used.
- The interpolation between two official data points is carried out using PRIMAP trends and rescaled ensuring the compiled series lies through all the official data points.
- If at least two non-missing official values are available, linear interpolation is performed.
- Extrapolation is executed by adding the PRIMAP level difference to the latest (or earliest) official point.
- Total, including land use, land-use change and forestry (LULUCF), is obtained by adding LULUCF and Total, excluding LULUCF estimates. The other remaining category levels are computed by multiplying the sectoral share with the total emissions estimates.

The methodology allows for the construction of a complete GHG emissions dataset from 1990 to 2022 covering the 198 UNFCCC Parties. It includes CO_2, N_2O, CH_4, SF6, NF3, HFCs, PFCs. Total GHGs are computed as a sum of the estimates of all gases and a breakdown by the six main IPCC categories: Energy, Industrial Process, Agriculture, LULUCF, Waste and Other is provided. Finally, the estimates are expressed in terms of several Assessment Reports: SAR, AR4, AR5, AR6. This was made possible by recording the Global Warming Potential (GWP) in which the data were reported, and by applying a mapping table containing conversion factors to calculate levels in all possible GWPs of individual gases.

Table A A.1. Official GHG emissions data availability per year, country level

Countries	Official data
Annex I OECD countries	1990-2022
Chile	1990-2020
Colombia	1990-2018
Costa Rica	1990-2017
Israel	1996, 2000, 2002-22
Korea	1990-2021
Mexico	1990-2019
OECD partner countries	Complete official data only for 2010
China (P.R. of)	1994, 2005, 2010, 2012, 2014
India	1994, 2000, 2010, 2016
Argentina	1990-2020
Peru	2008-19
Saudi Arabia	1990, 2000, 2010, 2012
South Africa	1990, 1994, 2000-2020
Brazil	1990-2016
Bulgaria	1990-2022
Croatia	1990-2022
Indonesia	1990-1994, 2000-16
Malta	1990-2022
Romania	1990-2022

Source: UNFCCC, GHG emissions inventory, BURs and (OECD, 2023[1]).

GHG emissions targets

To compare NDC emissions targets of countries, the OECD developed a methodology to estimate GHG emissions targets for 2030 as physical emissions targets (Pizarro et al., 2024[2]). The methodology is as follows:

If the country NDC target is defined for 2030 in physical terms (i.e. in tonnes of CO_2e), the target is maintained.

Otherwise, targets are put into physical emissions levels for 2030 by applying transformations to country-level data to derive 2030 emissions targets in physical terms; these include adjustments for GDP, population and other transformations presented in OECD (2024[2]).

Countries' NDC targets are not directly comparable due to differences in coverage of sectors, gases and GWP. For comparison, emissions and targets were adjusted to a common scope and AR6, and covering all GHGs as follows:

- For any given country, only the GHG emissions for the gases and sectors implied in its NDC are considered and converted into AR6.

- Physical targets in the scope reported by an individual country in their NDC are converted into physical AR6 targets by multiplying the target by the ratio of the country's total GHG emissions for 2022 in AR6 over the GHG emissions in the scope of the original target.
- GHG emissions outside of scope are imputed. This applies to China only as it uniquely covers CO_2 in its NDC. To this end, non-CO_2 gases are projected within a range. A lower bound assumes these gases are reduced at the same percentage as CO_2. An upper bound assumes these gases continue to maintain the same trend as in 2010-22.
- For non-IPAC countries, 2030 targets are calculated as a residual from global emissions (from UNEP, 2023), while 2050 targets are calculated as a residual considering only countries with no net-zero target.

To calculate emissions based on countries' net-zero targets, a complete achievement of these targets as presented was assumed. Global emissions for 2030 were taken from UNEP (2023[3]), with the 2030 value used for emissions under unconditional NDCs. In addition, 2050 emissions were projected based on the assumption of countries achieving their net-zero targets as proposed. Emissions for countries without a net-zero target were assumed to be at the same level as 2022, with a range of +/- 10% (e.g. Iran, Azerbaijan and others).

Moreover:

- EU-27 countries were considered as a bloc that reaches climate neutrality by 2050, as per the EU Law; individual countries' targets differ since some do not have a net-zero target.
- Emissions for countries with a net-zero target by later than 2050 are estimated based on a linear trajectory to their target year (e.g. China by 2060 and India by 2070).
- Emissions were adjusted based on differences in LULUCF estimates (according to (UNEP 2023[4]), differences among the bookkeeping method and national inventories were about 6.4 Gt CO_2e, assumed to remain constant by 2060). Projections are also adjusted by international aviation and shipping, which account for 4-5% of global emissions (IEA, 2023[10]). International aviation and shipping are assumed to be 0 by 2050 as per the international agreements by the International Air and Transport Association and the International Maritime Organization; this reduction is assumed to be linear from 2022 to 2050.
- GHG emissions for 2022 are calculated using data from PRIMAP and refined by the OECD. They refer to aggregate emissions for all 198 UNFCCC parties, including LULUCF; 2030 and 2050 emissions consistent with 1.5°C increase pathways were taken from UNEP (2023[3]).

Table A A.2. Detailed estimates of GHG emissions targets for 2030 and 2050 (Gt CO2e)

	2022	2030	2050
UNEP estimated global emissions under current policies*		57 (53-59)	56 (25-68)
Global emissions if targets achieved	55.5 (52-63)	55 (54-57)*	21.1 (18-24.7)
- LULUCF adjustments (outside inventories)	6.4 (5.2-7.6)	6.4 (5.2-7.6)	6.4 (5.2-7.6)
- International bunkers (aviation and maritime)	4.1	5.2 (4.7-5.7)	0
Total countries (in GHG invent., incl. LULUCF) if targets achieved	45.1	43 (41-45)	14.7 (12.6-16.8)
• **IPAC**	37.3	32.2 (31.6-32.8)	7.8 (7-8.6)
i. OECD	13.3	9.4	0.2 (0.1-0.3)
ii. IPAC non-OECD	24.2	22.7 (22.2-23.4)	7.5 (6.8-8.2)
• **Rest of the world**	7.6	10.7 (9.4-12.2)	7.0 (5.8-8.3)
1.5 °C consistent*		33 (26-34)	8 (5-13)
1.5 °C Emissions gap		22	13.2
2 °C Consistent*		41 (37-46)	20 (16-24)
2 °C Emissions gap		14	1.1

Source: *Projections taken from (UNEP, 2024[4]).

Note: LULUCF=land use, land-use change and forestry. Emissions are expressed in terms of Gt CO_2e, using AR6 GWP. Global emissions (in blue) equal total emissions of countries in national inventories (green) and emission adjustments for emissions not accounted in national inventories. Net-zero targets by 2050 assume the full implementation of the targets as presented. Emissions for countries without a net-zero pledge were calculated as a residual from business-as-usual emissions estimated by (UNEP, 2024[4]). EU-27 countries were considered as a bloc that reaches climate neutrality by 2050. Individual EU countries' targets commitments differ, however, since some do not have a national level net-zero target. Further details are available in Annex A.

Chapter 2

The OECD set of indicators is based on historical observational data – collected and recorded – that go back as far as 1979. This time period is relatively short for analysing climate change events. Nevertheless, the data, while limited, still show the exposure of climate-related hazards to the population, croplands, forests and urban areas.[2] These 44 years of data illustrate that climate change impacts are already visible by analysing even a short period of historical data [for a full discussion, see Maes et al. (2022[5])]. These indicators reflect what has happened, not what will happen (Box 2.1). Nevertheless, the dataset can support countries to understand the evolution and potential impact of climate-related hazards to guide policy choices.

Information on disaster events and their related costs has limitations due to inconsistent reporting by national governments and in international databases. The loss databases are essential to assess policy and monitor progress, but they are hardly ever mandated by national or supra-national legislations. There are several supra-national framework directives, but they remain vague when it comes to recording losses from disasters; their implementation would hugely benefit from the availability of such information.

No single database has complete coverage of losses from disaster events. For example, the United Nations Disaster Risk Reduction (UNDRR) DesInventar-Sendai database provides a common platform for countries to collect loss data on a national level; however, only ten OECD and OECD partner countries use this database to date (UNDRR, n.d.[6]).[3] It is especially difficult to quantify economic losses in harmonisation. Although definitions exist for calculating basic measurements of economic losses, such as affected buildings, agricultural assets and civil infrastructure, this is not consistently done for all disaster events across countries.[4] The threshold employed in a database to determine whether an extreme weather event is recorded is also significant; it can generate different results and comparability issues.[5]

Finally, methods for calculating losses exist in the context of estimating damages in the immediate aftermath of a disaster to anticipate the level of support required by the international community such as the Post-Disaster Needs Assessment (PDNA). To mainstream and standardise the PDNA, the United

Nations, the World Bank and the European Commission have jointly developed methodological guidelines. Physical damages and economic losses are evaluated using the Damage and Loss Assessment and human recovery needs are investigated through the Human Recovery Needs Assessment and a Recovery Framework. However, there is no central database to collect the results of PDNAs that had been conducted, except for the countries covered in DesInventar.

Chapter 3

The Climate Actions and Policies Measurement Framework (CAPMF) is an internationally harmonised climate policy database developed by the OECD. It is based on a structured policy typology that tracks a common set of policies with common definitions and harmonised policy attributes on an annual basis. The CAPMF complements other international policy tracking tools such as the reporting frameworks to the UNFCCC.

Based on 130 policy variables, the CAPMF tracks 56 climate actions and policies, which cover 75% of policies listed in the 2022 IPCC report, from 1990-2023 for 50 countries and the European Union. These countries are jointly responsible for over 63% of global GHG emissions. For each policy, the CAPMF measures policy stringency, defined as the degree to which policies incentivise emissions reductions. The CAPMF comprises climate-positive instruments (e.g. carbon taxes), as well as reform of climate-negative measures (e.g. reform of fossil fuel subsidies). The CAPMF also includes some climate-relevant policies such as air pollution standards, i.e. policies whose primary intent is not mitigation, but which have a material effect on emissions. While the focus of the CAPMF is on national climate action, it still includes key subnational policies such as subnational emissions trading schemes and renewable portfolio standards.

For *The Climate Action Monitor 2024*, missing policy data in 2023 were substituted by the last observed data in the last five years. This concerns 16% (9 of 56) of the policies captured by the CAPMF. Substituting the imputed data by the actual data once they become available is, unlikely to change the key results of Chapter 3. However, some messages may need to be refined, notably as country-level data on fossil fuel subsidies are not yet included.

The primary focus of the CAPMF is to track the evolution and stringency of mitigation policies over time (1990 to 2023). It collects a broad range of harmonised data that is internationally comparable and suitable for a broad-based quantitative and qualitative analysis. However, the CAPMF has some limitations as explained in the chapter and, hence, should be interpreted carefully (Nachtigall et al., 2022[7]).

Figure A A.1. Climate policy action rebounded in every sector except electricity

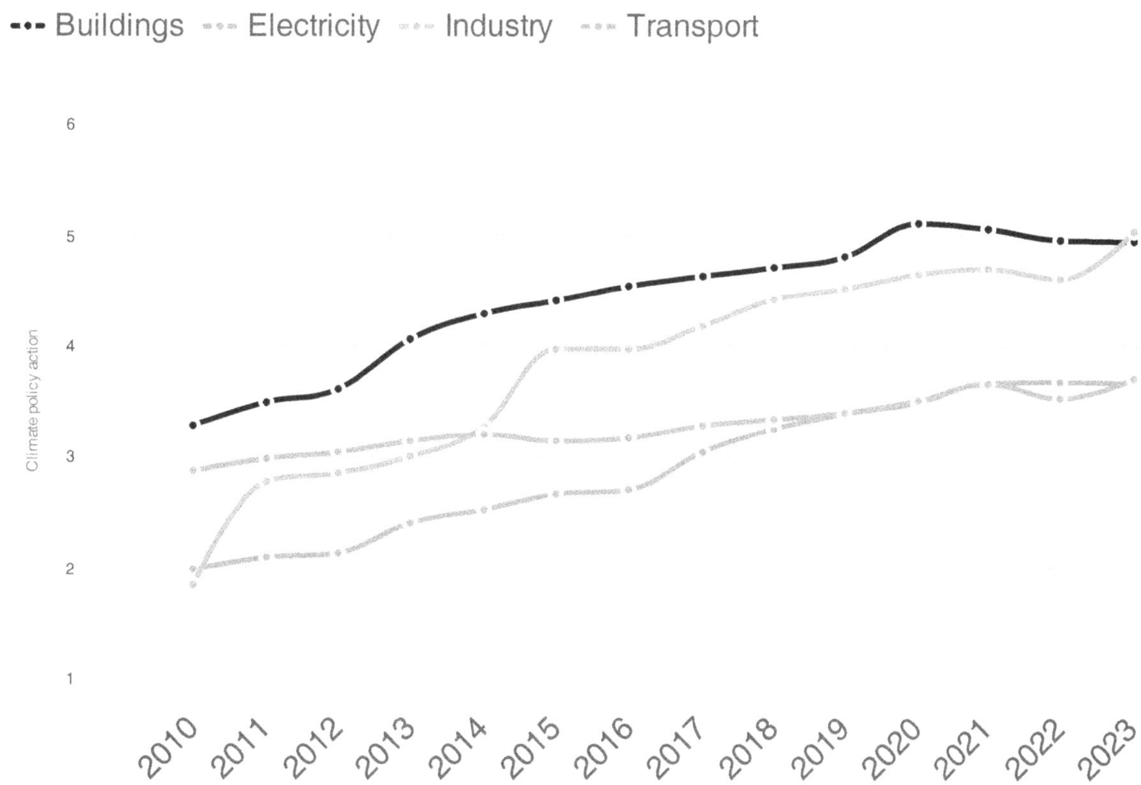

Note: Climate policy action is measured as a combination of policy adoption and policy stringency.

Source: Based on data from OECD, IEA, ITF, World Bank and others using the methodology of Nachtigall, D. et al. (2022): "The climate actions and policies measurement framework: A structured and harmonised climate policy database to monitor countries' mitigation action", *OECD Environment Working Papers*, No. 203, OECD Publishing, Paris, https://doi.org/10.1787/2caa60ce-en.

Figure A A.2. Electricity-related emissions kept on rising strongly

Emissions by sector (Index 2010=100), OECD and OECD partner countries, 2010-2022

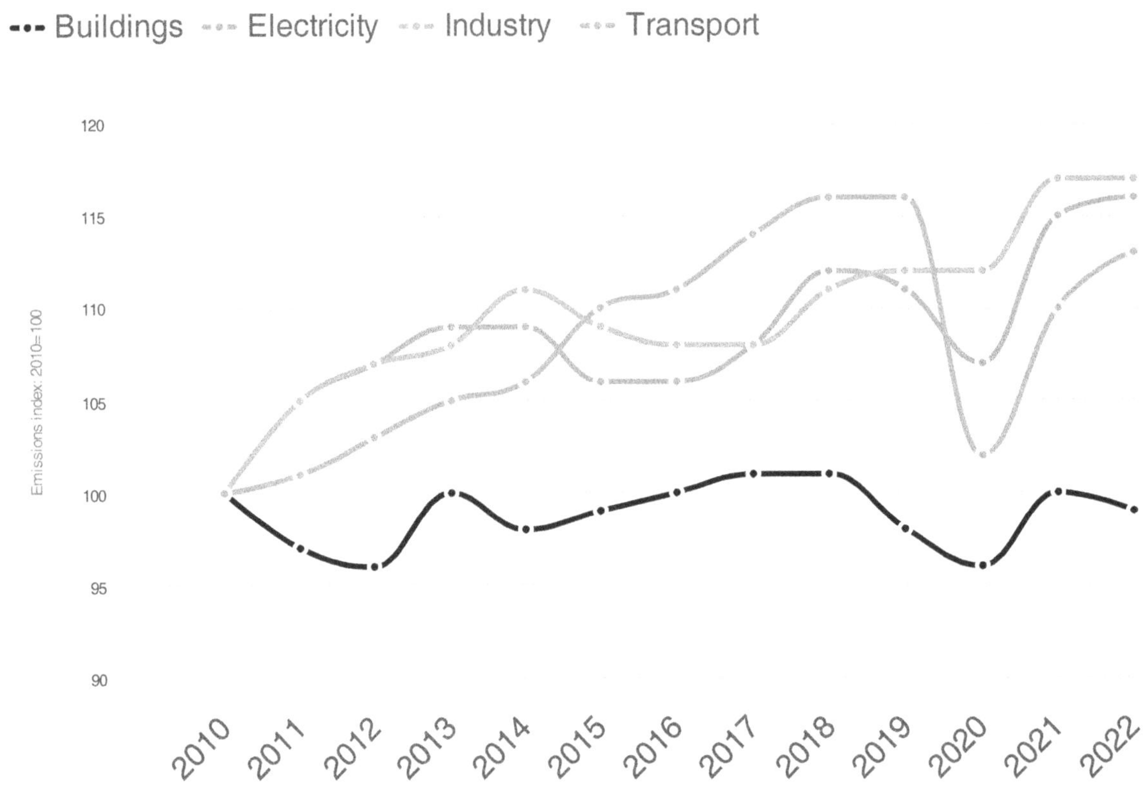

Source: Based on data from OECD, IEA, ITF, World Bank and others using the methodology of Nachtigall et al. (2022): "The climate actions and policies measurement framework: A structured and harmonised climate policy database to monitor countries' mitigation action", *OECD Environment Working Papers*, No. 203, OECD Publishing, Paris, https://doi.org/10.1787/2caa60ce-en. Emissions data are from European Commission, Joint Research Centre (JRC)/Netherlands Environmental Assessment Agency (PBL): Emission Database for Global Atmospheric Research (EDGAR).

Figure A A.3. Climate action grew for some policies but declined for others

Change in climate action between 2023 and 2022 by policy

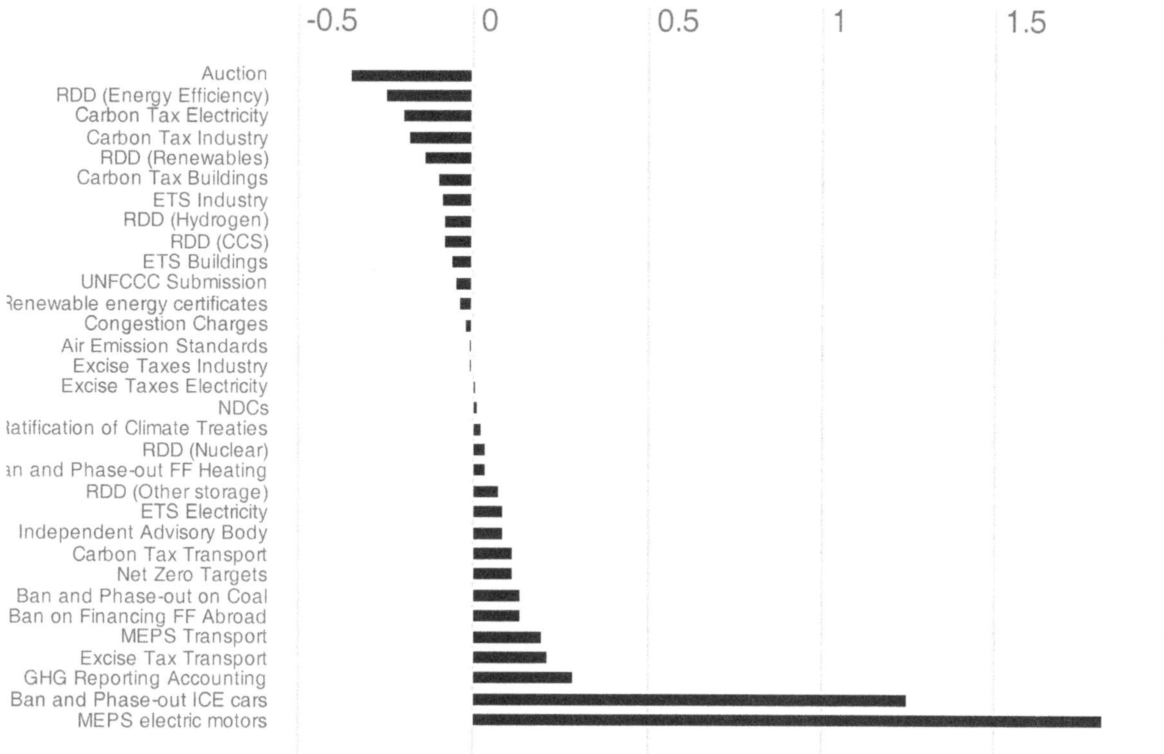

Note: Climate policy action is measured as a combination of policy adoption and policy stringency.

Source: Based on data from OECD, IEA, ITF, World Bank and others using the methodology of Nachtigall, D. et al. (2022): "The climate actions and policies measurement framework: A structured and harmonised climate policy database to monitor countries' mitigation action", *OECD Environment Working Papers*, No. 203, OECD Publishing, Paris, https://doi.org/10.1787/2caa60ce-en.

Figure A A.4. Fossil fuel subsidies receded in 2023 after reaching an all-time high in 2022

World fossil fuel consumption subsidies by fuel, billion USD, 2010-2023

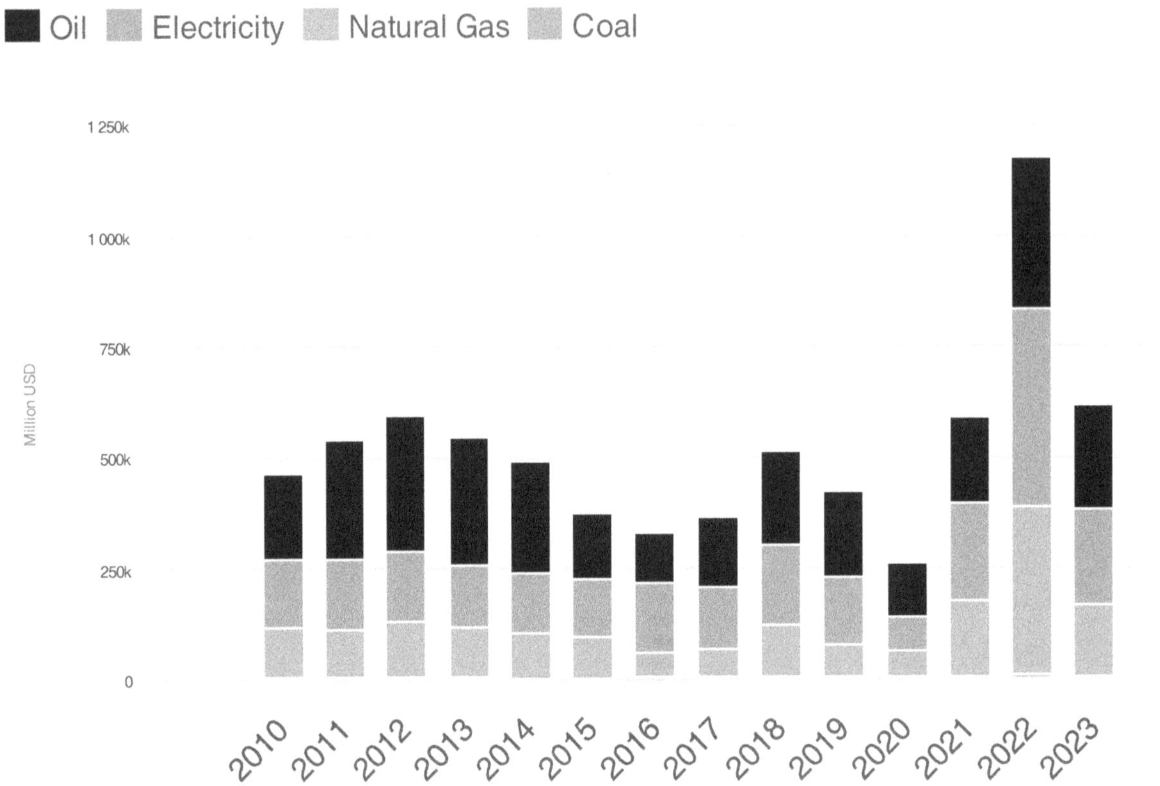

Source: IEA (2024), *Fossil fuels subsidies* (database), https://www.iea.org/topics/energy-subsidies.

Figure A A.5. The European Union further strengthened MEPS for electric motors

International Energy Efficiency (IE) class: 1990-2023, selected countries

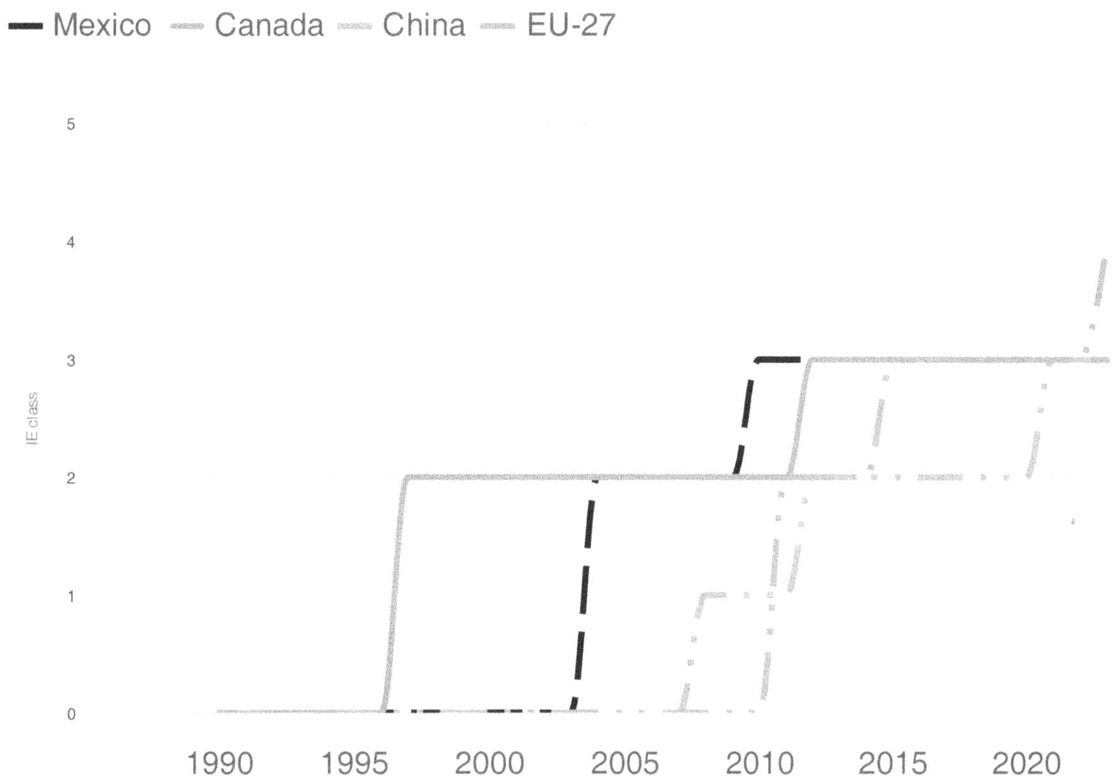

Source: Based on data from OECD, IEA, ITF, World Bank and others using the methodology of Nachtigall et al. (2022): "The climate actions and policies measurement framework: A structured and harmonised climate policy database to monitor countries' mitigation action", *OECD Environment Working Papers*, No. 203, OECD Publishing, Paris, https://doi.org/10.1787/2caa60ce-en

Figure A A.6. Developed countries exceeded the USD 100 billion goal of climate finance for the first time but two years later than the original target

Amounts provided and mobilised by developed countries, billion USD, 2013-2022

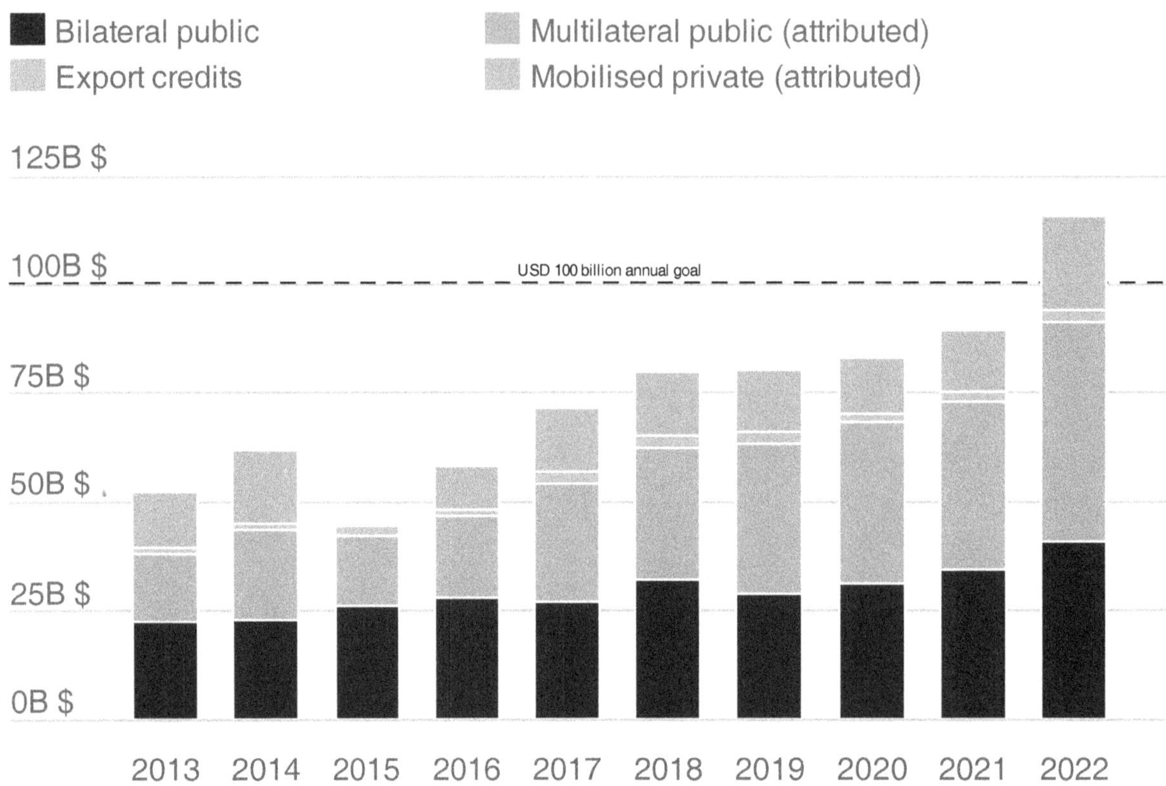

Note: The gap in the private finance series in 2015 is due to the implementation of enhanced measurement methodologies. As a result, private flows for 2016-22 cannot be directly compared with private flows for 2013-14.
Source: OECD (2024), *Climate Finance Provided and Mobilised by Developed Countries in 2013-2022*, Climate Finance and the USD 100 Billion Goal, OECD Publishing, Paris, https://doi.org/10.1787/19150727-en.

Figure A A.7. Countries choose different policy breadth and intensity

Policy adoption and average stringency of adopted policies, OECD and OECD partner countries, 2023

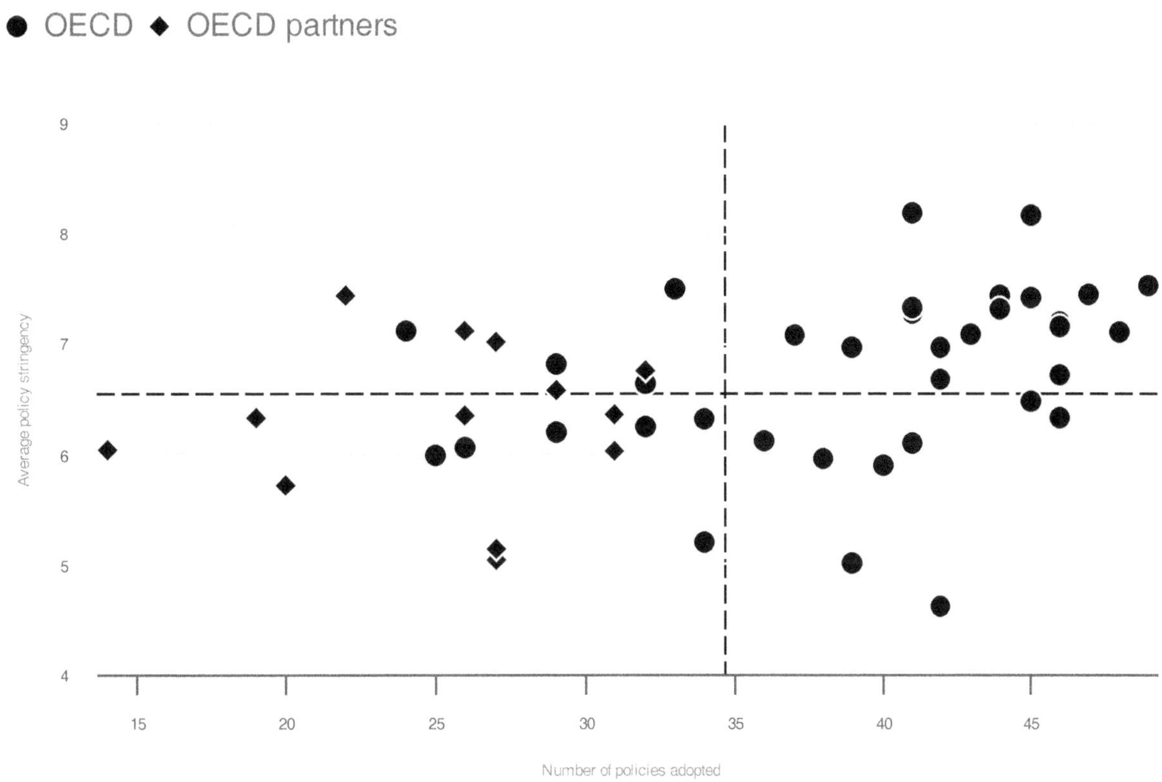

Source: Based on data from OECD, IEA, ITF, World Bank and others using the methodology of Nachtigall, D. et al. (2022): "The climate actions and policies measurement framework: A structured and harmonised climate policy database to monitor countries' mitigation action", Based on data from OECD, IEA, ITF, World Bank and others using the methodology of Nachtigall, D. et al. (2022): "The climate actions and policies measurement framework: A structured and harmonised climate policy database to monitor countries' mitigation action", *OECD Environment Working Papers*, No. 203, OECD Publishing, Paris, https://doi.org/10.1787/2caa60ce-en.

Figure A A.8. Climate policy action varies significantly across policy types and country groups

Climate policy action (0-10) by policy type and country group, 2023

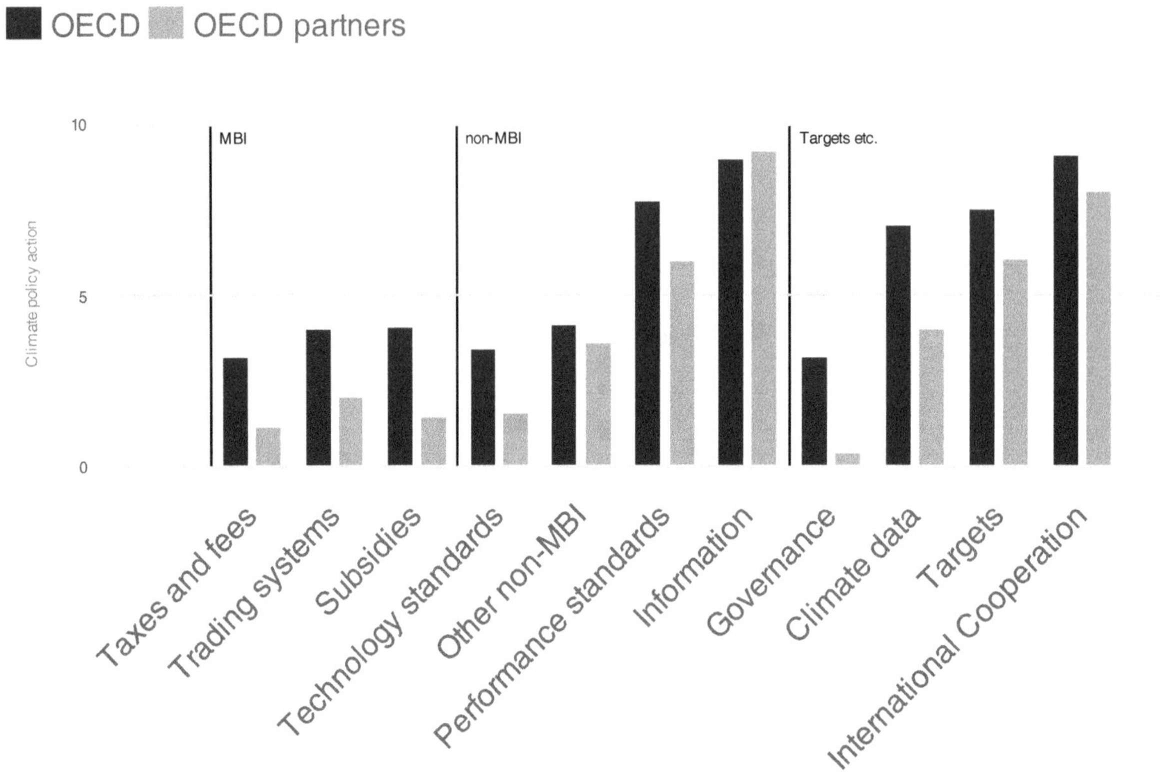

Source: Based on data from OECD, IEA, ITF, World Bank and others using the methodology of Nachtigall, D. et al. (2022): "The climate actions and policies measurement framework: A structured and harmonised climate policy database to monitor countries' mitigation action", *OECD Environment Working Papers*, No. 203, OECD Publishing, Paris, https://doi.org/10.1787/2caa60ce-en.

References

Dottori, F. et al. (2021), "A new dataset of river flood hazard maps for Europe and the Mediterranean Basin", *Earth System Climate Data*, Vol. 14/4, pp. 1549-1569, https://doi.org/10.5194/essd-14-1549-2022. [8]

Maes, M. et al. (2022), "Monitoring exposure to climate-related hazards: Indicator methodology and key results", *OECD Environment Working Papers*, No. 201, OECD Publishing, Paris, https://doi.org/10.1787/da074cb6-en. [5]

Nachtigall, D. et al. (2022), "The climate actions and policies measurement framework: A structured and harmonised climate policy database to monitor countries' mitigation action", *OECD Environment Working Papers*, No. 203, OECD Publishing, Paris, https://doi.org/10.1787/2caa60ce-en. [7]

OECD (2023), "Air and climate: Greenhouse gas emissions by source", *OECD Environment Statistics*, (database), https://www.oecd.org/en/data/indicators/air-and-ghg-emissions.html (accessed on 1 August 2024). [1]

Pizarro, R. et al. (2024), "GHG Emission Trends and Targets (GETT): Harmonised quantification methodology and indicators", *OECD Environment Working Papers*, No. 230, OECD Publishing, Paris, https://doi.org/10.1787/decef216-en. [2]

UNDRR (2019), *Global assessment report on disaster risk reduction 2019*, United Nations Office for Disaster Risk Reduction, Geneva, https://www.undrr.org/publication/global-assessment-report-disaster-risk-reduction-2019. [10]

UNDRR (n.d.), *United Nations DesInventar Open Source Initiative*, website, https://www.desinventar.net/ (accessed on 28 July 2023). [6]

UNEP (2024), *Emissions Gap Report 2024: No more hot air ... please! With a massive gap between rhetoric and reality, countries draft new climate commitments*, https://www.unep.org/emissions-gap-report-2024. [4]

UNEP (2023), *Emissions Gap Report 2023: Broken Record – Temperatures hit new highs, yet world fails to cut emissions (again)*, United Nations Environment Programme, https://doi.org/10.59117/20.500.11822/43922. [3]

WMO (2021), *Atlas of Mortality and Economic Losses from Weather, Climate and Water Extremes (1970–2019)*, https://library.wmo.int/index.php?lvl=notice_display&id=21930#.Y-5nmi_MLIU (accessed on 16 February 2023). [9]

Notes

[1] Additional data may be available through other sources such as national statistics websites. IPAC is exploring different alternatives to fill data gaps, including desk research to examine different sources and developing statistical methods.

[2] The development of this set of indicators is informed by standards from the World Meteorological Organization, the US National Ocean and Atmospheric Administration, latest research and standard developed by well-recognised organisations and builds on international frameworks for assessing climate-related hazards. Notwithstanding, over- or under-estimations of the actual exposure to climate-related hazards may occur. Further details on these limitations can be found in Maes et al. (2022[5]).

[3] Several databases gather secondary data on disaster occurrence and their human and economic cost. These include the EM-DAT database from the Centre for Research on the Epidemiology of Disasters' Emergency, hazard-specific databases (e.g. the Dartmouth Flood Observatory), actuaries and re-insurers (e.g. MunichRe's Natcat-SERVICE and SwissRe's Sigma databases). A weakness of such databases is the heterogeneous nature of the secondary data it relies upon; it often has problems with comparability across countries.

[4] For example, EM-DAT collects data on costs that accrue directly to assets, but it does not account for costs that accrue from business disruption in areas directly affected by the disaster; conversely, this is included in SwissRe's Sigma database. Beyond this, more intangible losses such as the impact on health or the environment, as well as cultural heritage loss and loss of reputation, are hardly ever accounted for due to difficulties in monetisation.

[5] For example, the WMO World Atlas report compares human loss figures from nationally reported data in two databases (DesInventar and EM-DAT) with different thresholds across Colombia, Ecuador, Indonesia and Niger (WMO, 2021[9]). It concluded that different threshold levels between the two databases did not affect the reporting of intensive (high-intensity, low-frequency) disasters (WMO, 2021[9]). However, the two databases had varying thresholds for extensive disasters (low-intensity, high-frequency), responsible for most economic losses from disasters (68.5% between 2005-17). Therefore, extensive disasters were sometimes included in one database but not the other (UNDRR, 2019[10]).

Glossary

Bans and phase-outs are regulatory instruments that mandate the cessation of the construction (ban) or the usage (phase-out) of certain activities.

CH_4 are methane emissions from solid waste, livestock, mining of hard coal and lignite, rice paddies, agriculture and leaks from natural gas pipelines.

Climate actions and policy instruments (or "policies") are policy instruments or other actions that have the explicit intent of achieving declared policy objectives to advance mitigation or are non-climate policies that are expected to have a material effect on GHG emissions. A policy is considered as adopted when it is effective in national legislation.

Climate actions and policies are divided into three types:

- Sectoral policies can be restricted to or are designed to apply to a specific source or economic sector.
- Cross-sectoral policies cut across more than one emission's source or sector. These are overarching policy areas to mitigate or remove domestic GHG emissions that cannot be easily attributed to a specific sector.
- International policies refer to commitments associated with international covenants or agreements where more than one country participates.

Climate-related extreme weather events are defined as a weather event resulting in 10 or more casualties, 100 or more affected people, the declaration of a state of emergency or a call for international assistance. Climate-related weather events include meteorological (extreme temperature, fog, storm), hydrological (wave action, landslide, flood) and climatological (wildfire, glacial lake outburst, drought). EM-DAT data cover both independent countries and dependent territories.

Coastal flooding threatens coastal regions and communities, affecting the population, built-up areas and other infrastructures. This indicator presents the annual percentage of the population exposed to coastal flooding with a 10, 25, 50 and 100-year return period. Data are expressed in percentages. Measuring population exposure to coastal flooding is possible using the World Bank coastal flood hazard maps (Muis et al., 2016), presenting a global re-analysis of storm surges and extreme sea-level events based on hydrodynamic modelling.

Extreme precipitation refers to a daily precipitation that exceeds the 99th percentile value over the reference period 1981-2010. Unlike a monthly approach, used for example for extreme temperature, percentiles are computed using all wet days of the reference period (i.e. 1981-2010) because the data sample would otherwise be too small to robustly compute seasonally adjusted percentiles. It defines a wet day as a day where total precipitation is above or equal to 1 mm. Since percentiles are computed using all wet days of the reference period in a given location, this implies a different occurrence frequency between different locations.

Demand-based GHG emissions encompass GHG emissions from the resident households of a country, as well as direct and indirect upstream emissions from its final expenditure of final goods and services.

Domestic material consumption (DMC) refers to the materials directly used in an economy, which refers to the apparent consumption of materials. DMC is computed as domestic extraction used minus exports plus imports.

Effective Carbon Rate (ECR) is the sum of fuel excise taxes, carbon taxes and tradeable permits that effectively put a price on carbon emissions. The **Net ECR** equals the ECR minus fossil fuel subsidies that decrease pre-tax fossil fuel prices.

Environmentally related taxes are compulsory, unrequited payments to government levied on tax bases deemed to be of environmental relevance, i.e. taxes that have a tax base with a proven, specific negative impact on the environment.

Fire danger is estimated with the Canadian Fire Weather Index (FWI), adjusted to account for biomass availability. Fire danger is defined as FWI values of 5 or higher, indicating very high or extreme fire danger.

Greenhouse gas (GHG) emissions refer to the sum of GHGs that have direct effects on climate change and are considered responsible for a major part of global warming: carbon dioxide (CO_2), methane (CH_4), nitrous oxide (N_2O), chlorofluorocarbons (CFCs), hydrofluorocarbons (HFCs), perfluorocarbons (PFCs), sulphur hexafluoride (SF_6) and nitrogen trifluoride (NF_3). They refer to GHGs emitted within the national territory and may include or exclude emissions and removals from land-use change and forestry. They do not cover international transactions of emissions reduction units or certified emissions reductions. GHG emissions estimates are divided into main sectors, which are groupings of related processes, sources and sinks.

Hot days are defined as those during which daily maximum temperature surpasses 35°C. Due to the resolution of the raw data, heat stress for small islands may be slightly underestimated. Several additional indicators also describe heat stress (such as the Universal Thermal Climate Index, or UTCI), which also takes moisture, wind and solar radiation into account); these should be considered for a more thorough analysis of exposure to heat for single countries.

Icing days are defined as days where the daily maximum temperature does not exceed 0°C.

Land exposure to cyclones: Category 1 cyclones on the Saffir-Simpson scale are described as "very dangerous winds that will produce some damage". Higher categories cover extensive, devastating and catastrophic damage, respectively. The return period is the average or estimated time that a specific climate-related hazard is likely to recur.

Paris Agreement long-term temperature goal: In Art. 2, the Paris Agreement, seeking to strengthen the global response to climate change, reaffirms the goal of limiting global temperature increase to well below 2°C, while pursuing efforts to limit the increase to 1.5°C.

Paris Agreement mitigation goal: In Art. 4, the Paris Agreement establishes binding commitments by all Parties to prepare, communicate and maintain a Nationally Determined Contribution (NDC) and to pursue domestic measures to achieve them. It also prescribes that Parties shall communicate their NDCs every five years and provide information necessary for clarity and transparency. To set a firm foundation for higher ambition, each successive NDC will represent a progression beyond the previous one and reflect the highest possible ambition. Developed countries should continue to take the lead through absolute economy-wide reduction targets. Meanwhile, developing countries should continue enhancing their mitigation efforts, and are encouraged to move towards economy-wide targets over time in the light of different national circumstances.

Policy approaches define countries' climate policy landscape. Policy approaches are the combination of countries' climate action (i.e. the number and stringency of its policies) and the types (e.g. market-based and non-market-based instruments) and areas (e.g. sectoral and cross-sectoral policies) of climate policies.

Policy instruments are institutional vehicles or tools through which governments facilitate the implementation of domestic and international objectives.

- **Market-based instruments** incentivise specific behaviour through a direct monetary transaction, influencing the prices or levels of production or consumption at the margin. Market-based instruments covered by the CAPMF include explicit (carbon taxes, emissions trading schemes) and implicit carbon pricing instruments (fuel excise taxes), among others.
- **Non-market-based instruments** seek to guide production or consumption decisions towards low-carbon alternatives through legal obligations, non-monetary incentives, enhanced information or enabling conditions (e.g. public transport infrastructure).

Policy stringency is the degree to which climate actions and policies incentivise or enable GHG emissions mitigation at home or abroad. The CAPMF calculates stringency as a relative concept by assigning a score between 0 (not stringent) and 10 (very stringent) for each policy variable based on the in-sample distribution across all countries and years of the policy variables' level (e.g. tax rate, emissions limit value, government expenditure).

Population and built-up area exposure to river flooding: River floods exposure indicators were computed using JRC River Flood Hazard Maps for Europe and the Mediterranean Basin region, and for the World (Dottori et al., 2021[8]). The maps depict flood-prone areas for river flood events for six different flood frequencies (from 1-in-10-years to 1-in-500-years). Cell values on these maps indicate the water depth (in m). For countries in Europe and around the Mediterranean Basin, the regional flood hazard maps were used, as the spatial resolution is higher (100 m) than the global maps (1 km). For the remaining countries, the global maps were used. To get flood-prone areas, a threshold of 1 cm was applied on the water depth. The return period is the average or estimated time that a specific climate-related hazard is likely to recur.

Production-based GHG emissions are estimated according to the residence principle. They refer to the GHG emitted from the resident economic activities and households of a country.

Soil moisture anomaly in cropland is a suitable indicator for monitoring the intensity of droughts and shows similar performances in identifying droughts to the Standardized Precipitation Index. Copernicus CDS ERA5-Land monthly averaged data and Copernicus global land cover data are used to calculate average cropland soil moisture anomaly.

Total energy supply (TES), or total primary energy supply, is made up of production + imports - exports - international marine bunkers - international aviation bunkers ± stock changes. Primary energy comprises coal, peat and peat products, oil shale, natural gas, crude oil and oil products, nuclear and renewable energy (bioenergy, geothermal, hydropower, ocean, solar and wind). Electricity trade is included in TES but excluded from the calculation of the breakdown by source.

Tropical nights are defined as nights where the minimum temperature does not fall below 20°C. Due to the resolution of the raw data, heat stress for small islands may be slightly underestimated. Several additional indicators describe heat stress (such as the Universal Thermal Climate Index), which also takes moisture, wind and solar radiation into account; these should be considered for a more thorough analysis of exposure to heat for single countries.

www.ingramcontent.com/pod-product-compliance
Lightning Source LLC
Chambersburg PA
CBHW061223240926
51846CB00006B/1338
9789264710313